John J. C. Abbott

The Insolvent Act of 1864

With Notes, Together with the Rules of Practice and the Tariff of Fees for

Lower Canada

John J. C. Abbott

The Insolvent Act of 1864
With Notes, Together with the Rules of Practice and the Tariff of Fees for Lower Canada

ISBN/EAN: 9783337159528

Printed in Europe, USA, Canada, Australia, Japan

Cover: Foto ©Suzi / pixelio.de

More available books at **www.hansebooks.com**

THE

INSOLVENT ACT OF 1864,

WITH NOTES

TOGETHER WITH

THE RULES OF PRACTICE

AND

THE TARIFF OF FEES FOR LOWER CANADA.

———

BY

THE HONORABLE J. J. C. ABBOTT, Q. C., M. P. P.

———

QUEBEC:
PRINTED BY GEORGE DESBARATS AND MALCOLM CAMERON,
Printer to the Queen's Most Excellent Majesty.

———

1864.

TO THE HONORABLE

MR. JUSTICE MEREDITH,

.

THIS LITTLE MANUAL IS RESPECTFULLY INSCRIBED

BY ONE WHO WAS FORMERLY HIS STUDENT,

.

IN GRATEFUL REMEMBRANCE OF MANY KINDNESSES.

PREFACE.

There has been for some years past an urgent demand in Canada, for a law creating a summary mode of realizing and distributing the estates of Insolvents, and of affording relief from liability, to debtors making a full disclosure and delivery of their estates to their Creditors. The absence of such a law, left to the failing debtor no chance of success in any future enterprise, unless he could succeed in the almost hopeless task, of procuring a discharge from every one of his creditors.

Thus many such were tempted to secure their remaining assets by dishonest devices, rather than leave themselves destitute by resigning them to their Creditors.

Whether the present law will reach the evils that have acquired such considerable proportions, or afford that relief to unfortunate debtors which they are entitled to in other commercial countries, remains to be seen. And however successful it may prove to be, there will doubtless be many particulars in which amendments to it will be required, to enable it to be worked effectually as to the objects sought to be attained by it, and harmoniously as regards the existing laws of the two provinces.

Having always felt a strong interest in the improvement of our commercial law, and given some attention to the subject of Bankrupt Laws generally and to the present Act in particular, I have naturally been desirous that the Insolvent Act of 1864 should receive a fair trial. And the more so that it embodies the idea I have always entertained that we should engraft upon our existing systems of law, such further procedure as may be required to expropriate and distribute the effects of an insolvent, and to discharge him from liability; rather than to create new and separate tribunals and proceedings for those purposes only.

I have therefore thrown together the notes to be found in this little volume, in the hope that they may serve to facilitate the application and use of the new statute. In preparing them I have seldom

ventured to offer an opinion upon the construction of clauses of
doubtful meaning. I have confined myself chiefly to the attempt
to point out the relations between different portions of the Act,
and their bearing upon each other—and to indicate where, in the
English, French, and Scotch, Bankrupt Laws, and in the leading
works upon them, analogous provisions and decisions may be
found. Before long the light afforded by judicial decisions upon
its clauses, will render the path of the commentator more easy and
more safe. In the meantime, however, I trust that the materials
collected in the following pages may be found not to be without
value, in the investigation of the true scope and meaning of the
Act. And although I feel that after the expenditure of considerable
labor I have achieved but little ; I venture to hope, that the little I
have been able to do, may prove in some degree useful and
acceptable.

                                              J. J. C. ABBOTT.

Montreal, October, 1864.

EDITIONS.

Doria and Macrae,—The Law and Practice of Bank-
    ruptcy .... D. & M........ **1863**
Denisart,—Collection de Décisions............... Anc. Den.. ....
Broderip and Bingham's Reports.... ....Brod. & Bing...
Taunton's Reports............................. Taunt....... ...
Modern Reports.. .... Mod......... ..
Comyn's Digest .... Com. Dig......
Lower Canada Reports.. .... L. C. Rep.....
The Lower Canada Jurist....................... L. C. Jur.. ....
La Loi du 28 Mai, 1838........................ C. Com... .....
The Bankruptcy (Scotland) Act 1856.. ....S. Act.........
The Bankruptcy Act 1861 (England) 24 & 25 Vict.
    cap. 134................................. E. Act.........
The Consolidated Statutes of Lower Canada... ...Cons. Stat. L. C.
The Consolidated Statutes of Canada..............Cons. Stat. Can.
Meeson & Welsby's Reports..................... M. & W.......
Barnwell and Cresswell's Reports.... .... B. & C........
Bingham's Reports............................ Bing..........
Louisiana Reports .... Louis.........
Denison's Crown cases........ ....Den. C. C......

THE

INSOLVENT ACT

OF 1864.

An Act respecting Insolvency.

WHEREAS it is expedient that provision be made for the settlement of the estates of insolvent debtors, for giving effect to arrangements between them and their creditors, and for the punishment of fraud : Therefore, Her Majesty, by and with the advice and consent of the Legislative Council and Assembly of Canada, enacts as follows : Preamble.

1. This Act shall apply in Lower Canada to traders only, and in Upper Canada to all persons whether traders or non-traders. Application of this Act.

1. By this section the operation of the Statute is limited in Lower Canada to traders.

In the legislation of France the test of the competency of a commercial Tribunal has sometimes consisted in the nature of the transaction brought before it, while at others, to give it jurisdiction, not only the transaction but the persons engaged in it were required to have a commercial character. The *Lettres Patentes* issued by Philip de Valois creating a commercial Tribunal in Brie and Champagne ; the Edict of Charles VII establishing the *Conservateurs de Lyon* in 1419 ; the Ordinance of Henry II in 1549 authorizing the election of Consular Judges in Toulouse ; the Edict of November, 1563, afterwards peremptorily enforced by declaratory Edicts in 1565 and 1611 ; with numerous others of a similar character, all require in general, that a transaction to be cognisable by the commercial Tribunals, should not only be in itself a commercial act, but should have taken place between persons engaged in commerce.

The Ordinance of 1673 follows the same system—Ord. 1673, tit. XII, arts. 2 to 10, Jousse, Ord. 1673, pp. 184 and seq. But the modern Code de Commerce appears sometimes to render the nature of the transaction the principal test of the jurisdiction of the tribunal.—Arts. 631, 636, 637, 638.

The jurisdiction created by the previous legislation may therefore be called personal, from the fact that the quality of the person was essential to

1

its existence ; in contradistinction to that established by the Code de Commerce, which is susceptible of being sustained in some cases by the commercial character of the person, without reference to the transaction ; and in others, by the commercial character of the transaction, independently of the persons engaged in it. The latter jurisdiction may therefore be considered at once personal and real ; personal, because the quality of a trader creates a presumption that his contracts are connected with his trade, leaving him to establish the contrary, while the contracts of a non trader are presumed to follow his quality, unless they are essentially of a commercial character ; and real, because he who enters into a contract which the law recognizes as essentially commercial, becomes in respect of that contract, amenable to the commercial Tribunals, whatever may be his quality. 4 Locré, pp. 93 and seq. ; 1 Pardessus, pp. 69 and seq., Nos. 48 and seq. ; 5 Pardessus, pp. 12 and seq., Nos. 1345 and seq.

In England there have not been of late any tribunals created for the regulation of commercial matters solely. But an exceptional jurisdiction for bankrupts has long existed there, which was purely commercial, inasmuch as until lately only traders could become bankrupt. But while the tribunal was commercial, its jurisdiction was personal, for the character of the debt upon which a creditor might base proceedings in bankruptcy, appears to have been held to be of no importance, even while the operation of the Statutes of Bankruptcy was limited to traders. Archbold, on Bankruptcy, p. 87, and the cases there cited.

The intention of this Act appears to be like that of the English Statute, to create a species of jurisdiction purely personal.

There is no limitation of its application to debts of a commercial character—but only in Lower Canada—and as respects one mode of proceeding, in Upper Canada—to persons who are traders ;—the nature of the debts, upon which proceedings may be adopted under it, being in most cases a matter of indifference. The jurisdiction it creates is therefore purely personal.

But though the operation of the Statute is thus restricted, it contains no definition of the term used to describe the class of persons who are made specially subject to its provisions.

The question, who is a trader ? becomes therefore of the utmost importance in every case in Lower Canada, and in many cases in Upper Canada. And the replies to it must be based upon the different laws which prevail respectively in these two sections of the province.

With regard to Upper Canada, which receives from England the basis of its system of law, it may be remarked that the question under consideration appears generally to have been examined in the mother country as an incident to the operation of the Bankrupt laws, and it is therefore chiefly with reference to the law of bankruptcy that the word " trader" has acquired a distinct and precise legal signification in England.

The earlier English statutes, though they did not use the word " trader", attempted a definition or description of the persons who might fall within the operation of their provisions. Thus, the 13 Eliz., cap. 7 ; 1 Jac. I, cap. 15, and the 21 Jac. I, cap. 19, provided that every one who used the trade of merchandise by bargaining, &c., or sought his living by buying and selling, was liable to become bankrupt. And a person was held to be included within this definition though he did not sell the wares that he bought, but converted them into saleable commodities which he afterwards sold. In other words an artisan who purchased materials to be used in making articles for sale was held to be within the statute. Ld. Raymond, 741 ; 4 Burr., 2148.

But it was also held that to bring a person within these statutes his principal means of living must have been gained, or at least sought to be gained by some occupation which fell within their purview. 1 T. Rep. 573, 2 Blk., 476.

The 12 and 14 Car. II, cap. 21, is the first statute in which the word " trader" is used. But the 6 Geo. IV, cap. 16, and subsequent Bankruptcy statutes adopt it as a term in use and well understood ; and in the jurisprudence which commenced to grow up under the early statutes and has continued to prevail to the present day, it is used as a generic term descriptive of the class of persons liable to become bankrupt.

The recent English statutes, commencing with the 6 Geo. IV, cap. 16, contain a specific list or denomination of the persons liable as traders to be made bankrupt ; a sweeping clause bringing within their provisions all persons previously liable as traders to the Bankrupt laws ; and a description or definition, in general terms, very similar to those of the older statutes, of the kind of occupation which made persons so liable. The distinction between the persons to whom the specific denominations are applicable, and those only falling within the general description of classes, is this ; that the former come within the Act, however little business they may transact in that capacity ; but the other classes only come within it, if their business holds a prominent position in their avowed or actual means of living. 1 Doria & Macrae, on Bankruptcy, p. 84. The definition of trading, which is given by the statutes of Elizabeth and James is therefore still correct so far as it goes : and a very considerable number of cases illustrative of its bearing—and of the distinctions which have arisen upon it, and upon subsequent, but similar legislation, are collected in 1 Doria & Macrae, pp. 100 and seq.; and in Archbold on Bankrpptcy, pp. 39, 40. The doctrine on this subject is thus summed up by the former at p. 100. Assuming that the occupation under consideration is in itself of the nature of trade—they say that, " to constitute a trading in law, there must be a substantive and " independent trading ; a general intention to trade," (or rather an intention to trade generally) ; " and a trading as the means of gaining a livelihood."

This of course only applies to the general definition or description of a trader or person subject to become bankrupt, enacted in the earlier statutes of Bankruptcy and retained in the more recent ones, and not to the specific denominations which are also detailed in the latter ; and it is in accordance with the idea conveyed by the word " trader" in its ordinary acceptation. While these specific denominations therefore may not fall within the provisions of this Act, except in so far as their characteristics may satisfy that general definition or description, there would seem to be no good reason why those and all other cases which do so satisfy it, should not, in Upper Canada, be held to be within this statute. And if so, the thorough examination which the subject has received in England, first upon the definitions contained in the Statutes of Elizabeth and James, and afterwards upon the portion of the more recent Statutes in which that definition is retained ; and the multitude of adjudged cases settling every point upon which difficulty could arise, will probably render it easy in Upper Canada to distinguish between traders and non-traders whenever the statute requires such distinction to be made. And it may be well in this connection to notice the opinion of Mr. Smith, (Mer. Law, p. 1), that the word " trader" would receive in general a somewhat wider construction than the Bankrupt Statutes seem to justify, if it be used without reference to those statutes.

In France no definitions of the various terms used to describe the class of persons subject to Consular jurisdiction, are to be found in the older legislation. And moreover there was not formerly any phrase or word like the word " trader" in England, universally adopted as descriptive of that class, or as comprising within its technical meaning the various trades or occupations which made those who practised them amenable to the Commercial Tribunals. But a short examination of the powers of some of the most important of those Courts, will enable a tolerably exact idea to be attained, of the quality of the persons, and the nature of the transactions subjected to their jurisdiction. And thus the quality of the persons whom the law of Lower Canada would regard as being comprised within the designation of traders may also eventually be arrived at.

The famous tribunal of the *Conservateurs de Lyon*, is said to have been the model upon which the Consular Courts were afterwards formed. The jurisdiction of this tribunal seems to have been extensive, and to comprise the right of trying all causes of which the subject matter was of a commercial character, provided the parties, or as it would appear by the declaration of 1669, one of the parties was a " *marchand ou négociant*."—

1 *

(See Edit of Charles VII, 1419, and the subsequent declaration of August, 1699, *post*.)

The Ord. of Henri II, 1549, authorizing the merchants of Toulouse to elect a prior and two consuls, gave to the tribunal so created, jurisdiction to decide all cases which might arise, " *pour raison de marchandises, foires " et assurances entre les marchands et fabricants de Toulouse.*"

The Ord. of 1563, Art. 6, gives to *juges consuls* jurisdiction, "*pour connaître des marchands, et de tous procès et différends qui seront ci-après mûs entre marchands et pour fait de marchandises seulement, leurs veuves marchandes publiques, leurs facteurs, serviteurs et commettants, tous marchands.*" These expressions would seem to limit the consular power to a comparatively small class of those persons who are certainly traders—but the remainder of the article shews plainly that such was not the intention of the law. For it goes on to say : *soit que les différends procèdent d'obligations, cédules, récépissés, lettres de change ou de crédit, réponses, assurances, transports de dettes et novations d'icelles, calculs ou erreurs en iceux, compagnies, sociétés ou associations déjà faites, ou qui se feront ci-après.* This description of the transactions which may be comprised within the phrase, *pour fait de marchandises*, shews that the word *marchand* and *marchandises* have in this Ordinance a wider signification than that which belongs to the words merchants and merchandise—and that as therein used, the word *marchand* approximates closely to the word *commerçant*—which afterwards came into use as a generic term comprising all kinds of persons engaged in trade, and subjected by reason of their quality to the jurisdiction of the commercial Tribunals. And this interpretation of these phrases may be fully sustained by authority. Jousse sur l'Ord. de 1673, tit. 1, art. 6,— tit. 12, art. 1 ; 1 Savary parf. neg., p. 214 ; 1 Pardessus, pp. 8 et seq., Nos. 8 et seq. ; 1 Vincent, 127 ; Orillard, No. 121.

And the phrase *pour fait de marchandises* used in the sense in which it appears in the Ord. of 1563, seems to have been of frequent occurrence in the official documents creating or defining the powers of Commercial Courts, by whatever name they might be called. (See the various Edicts, Ordinances and Declarations on this subject—most of which are referred to in 1 Toubeau, Liv. 1, Tit. XIII.)

A Declaration of the 8th August, 1572, made with reference to the town of Tours, &c., uses nearly the same form of expression as the Ordinance of 1563.

Again, by a Declaration of the 29th March, 1623, having reference to consular jurisdiction generally, it was ordered *que tous marchands, voituriers, négociateurs, procéderont par-devant les juges et consuls.*

By an Edict of the 13th August, 1669, passed for the purpose of settling difficulties as to conflicting jurisdictions which had arisen between the ordinary and Commercial Tribunals at Lyons, it was declared with reference to the *Conservateur*, or *Prévôt des Marchands : qu'il connaîtra de toutes affaires entre marchands et négociants en gros et en détail, manufacturiers des choses servant au négoce et autres de quelle qualité et condition qu'ils soient, pourrû que l'une des parties soit marchand ou négociant, et que ce soit pour fait de négoce, marchandise ou manufacture.* And by the same Edict, those, amongst others, who sell merchandise, or buy it to sell again, are declared amenable to the jurisdiction of the *Conservateurs.*

In the famous Ord. of 1673, there is a greater amplitude of detail as to the persons amenable to the Consular tribunals, than is to be found in any of the earlier acts of legislation taken separately—but in reality it merely embodies what may be gathered from the whole of the previous *actes, déclarations* and *ordonnances* taken together. Unity of purpose is perceptible enough running through the various official documents relating to the commercial jurisdiction, extracts from some of which have been cited, though the mode of expressing that purpose is different in many of them, and defective in nearly all. The Ord. of 1673 therefore was made to convey what was no doubt the intention of all, though somewhat more than was expressed in any one of the legislative or *quasi* legislative acts which preceded it. And it has been considered to be explanatory of the Ordinance of 1563, and declaratory in most respects of the law as it existed at the time of its passage.

By this ordinance the *juges consuls* were empowered to take cognizance of all Bills of Exchange and sales of merchandise, between *marchands et négociants;* commissions and charges of commercial agents connected with traffic; insurances and other contracts connected with maritime trade; and also sales made to *artisans et gens de métier* of merchandise to be sold again, or to be used in their trade. It would appear that bankers also were subject to the same jurisdiction. And as it has been shewn that these tribunals were purely commercial, only taking cognizance of commercial transactions; it may be said that the sanction of the law is plainly given for describing the species of transactions referred to in the articles cited from the Ord. of 1673, as *actes de commerce,* or, as our Ordinance (25 Geo. III, cap. 2,) terms them, " Commercial Matters;" and that those who enter into such transactions; habitually or in the language of the English Statutes " seek their living " by so doing, may without impropriety be styled *commerçants* or traders.

The terms of the articles regulating this subject are as follows:

Art. 2. " Les juges-consuls connaîtront de tous billets de change faits " entre négociants et marchands, ou dont ils devront la valeur, et entre " toutes personnes pour lettres de change ou remises d'argent de place en " place."

Art. 4. " Ils connaîtront les différends pour ventes faites par des mar- " chands, artisans et gens do métier afin de revendre ou de travailler de " leur profession, comme à tailleurs d'habits pour étoffes, etc., etc., ' * ' et " autres semblables.

Art. 5. " Connaîtront aussi des gages, salaires, et pensions des commis- " sionnaires, facteurs ou servi eurs des marchands pour le fait du trafic " seulement."

Art. 7. " Connaîtront des différends à cause des assurances, grosses " aventures, promesses, obligations et contrats concernant le commerce de " la mer, le fret et le naulage des vaisseaux."

See also Tit. 2, Art. 6.

Without seeking further to investigate the law of France on the subject under consideration, it would not be difficult to discover from the Legislation and Jurisprudence previous to 1673; a great portion of which might be cited as law in Lower Canada; what must have been the nature of a man's occupation to cause him to be subjected to consular jurisdiction. But if further and authoritative aid can be obtained in the development of this subject, it is expedient that it should be sought for and made use of.

It has been already attempted to be shewn, and it will be hereafter assumed to be the fact, that the Ord. of 1673, converted no act previously non-commercial, into a commercial act, but merely collected and grouped the numerous transactions that previous enactments and the judgments of of the Courts had characterized as commercial; and gave to the jurisprudence so created the sanction of authority. That this assumption is essentially correct, will not, it is believed, be much controverted in Lower Canada; and if it were, it could be supported if not established, by an array of citations much too extensive for the present note.

But while the terms of this ordinance and the commentaries of various laborious and learned writers upon it, are of the utmost importance in this investigation, there is yet available, later, more elaborate d and more complete, authoritative *dicta,* in the articles of the *code de commerce* appropriate to the subject. And the numerous and learned writers upon the code have been able to bring the light of modern experience, and aid the modern facilities for research, to bear upon the development of its provisions. In articles 1, 632 and 633, of that code, " traders " and commercial transactions are defined and described.

Art. 1. Enacts as follows:

" Sont commerçants, ceux qui exercent des actes de commerce, et en font " leur profession habituelle."

And articles 632 and 633, thus describe what are to be held in law to be *actes de commerce :*

Art. 632. "La loi répute acte de commerce tout achat de denrées et
" marchandises pour les revendre, soit en nature, soit après les avcir travail-
" lées et mises en œuvre, ou même pour en louer simplement l'usage. Toute
" entreprise de manufactures, de commission, de transport par terre ou par
" eau."

" Toute entreprise de fournitures, d'agences, bureaux d'affaires, établisse-
" ment de ventes à l'encan, de spectacles publics ;
" Toute opération de change, banque ou courtage ;
" Toutes les opérations de banques publiques ;
" Toutes obligations entre négociants, marchands et banquiers ;
" Entre toutes personnes, les lettres de change, ou remises d'argent faites
" de place en place."

Art. 633. " La loi répute pareillement acte de commerce, toute entreprise
" de construction, et tous achats, ventes et reventes de bâtiments pour la
" navigation intérieure ;
" Toutes expéditions maritimes ;
" Tout achat ou vente d'agrès, apparaux et avitaillements ;
" Tout affrétement ou nolissement, emprunt ou prêt à la grosse ; toutes
" assurances ou autres contrats concernant le commerce de la mer ;
" Tous accords et conventions pour salaires et loyers d'équipages ;
" Tous engagements de gens de mer pour le service de bâtiments de
" commerce."

If these definitions introduced no new principle into the commercial law
of France ; but constituted merely the result of the labours of the learned
men to whom the code owes its origin, in their search for a concise and clear
description of the classes of persons and of transactions previously subject
to the consular jurisdiction and about to be rendered amenable to similar
tribunals under a different name ; they may be adopted here as correct expo-
nents of the law as to the classes of persons subject to the present Act, and
as to the classes of transactions, the practice of which will bring persons
within its provisions. And the comments upon them of such men as Pardessus and Massé will receive a character of authority which will greatly
facilitate the decision of any questions that may arise upon the terms of this
clause of our statute.

If on the other hand these definitions are mere arbitrary enactments,
having no foundation in the old law, they cease to be of interest in this behalf,
and render it necessary to confine the enquiry, to the state of the law previous to their promulgation.

It is contended, however, and with much reason, that in many respects,
and specially in respect of those matters legislated upon by the three above
cited articles, the *code de commerce* did not change in any material degree
the ancient law. (Bécane sur Jousse, com. de l'ord. de 1673, pp. 288, 305,
in notis. 1 Vincens, p. 121. Orillard, No. 181 ; Merlin, Rep. vo. Marchandises, fait de, Pozer vs Meiklejohn, Pyke, p. 11.)

And any one may verify the correctness of the assertions of these writers
by comparing, in the arrêts and judgments of the respective periods, the
persons and acts that have been adjudged under the ancient legislation and
under the code respectively, to be *justiciables* by the commercial tribunals.

The essential elements of the definitions of the generic terms *commerçant*
and *acte de commerce* which are given by the code, may be gathered from
previous legislation, and from the jurisprudence which prevailed previous to
its enactment. Long before that time the word *commerçant* had begun to be
used as descriptive of persons amenable to Commercial tribunals. 1 Toubeau,
p. 260. Salté sur l'ord. de 1673, pp. 415, 416, 438, Anc. Den. vo. *commerçans ;* Rogron, jur. com. *passim.* Nicodeme Ex. des Com. And the sense in
which it is so used seems to accord precisely with the definition given of it
by the code.

In fact the *Code de Commerce* appears to have performed in its turn,
that which was done with respect to a previous age by the Ord. of 1673 ;
and although the progress and extension of trade, rendered expedient greater
detail, no change was operated in the principles which should regulate
the classification of a transaction or of a person as being commercial or
non-commercial.

Assuming then what it is believed might easily be more fully demonstrated, that the definitions given by the Code de Commerce of *commerçants* and of *actes de commerce*, are only developments of principles which are to be found in the ancient legislation and jurisprudence, and correctly express those principles ; the commentators on the Code become valuable auxiliaries in the investigation of the true construction of the first of those expressions, which is used in our statute to designate those persons specially subject to its provisions.

" Le commerce," says Massé, " envisagé sous un point de vue général est donc une communication réciproque entre deux personnes, dont l'une donne à l'autre une chose pour une autre chose qu'elle en reçoit. Mais lorsque ces rapports intéressés ont lieu avec suite et fréquemment entre personnes dont, soit l'une ou l'autre, soit toutes les deux, se proposent un profit qui doit être le résultat des communications établies entre elles, alors ce commerce est d'une espèce particulière, et constitue le commerce proprement dit. *Finis mercatorum est lucrum.* En ce sens plus restreint et plus usuel, le commerce consiste donc dans une spéculation où l'on achète afin de revendre—et ou l'on vend ce qu'on a acheté pour le revendre ; ou mieux encore, dans les diverses négociations qui ont pour objet d'opérer ou de faciliter les échanges des produits de la nature ou de l'industrie à l'effet d'en tirer quelque profit." 1 Massé, Droit Com., pp. 3, 4.

The latter part of this definition is taken *verbatim* from Pardessus, 1 Pard. droit com., p. 1.

It would be impossible within the limits of the present note to follow the developments of this definition by M. Massé, or his discussion of the various *Actes de Commerce* detailed in art. 632 and 633 of the Code. He appears to have desired to shew that the legislation which constituted these transactions, *Actes de Commerce*, was not purely arbitrary, but was based upon principle and upon authority—and it is difficult to read his lucid and logical treatise without being of opinion that he has succeeded in doing so. His opinion therefore also supports the position that the *Code de Commerce* enacted no new thing in its definitions of traders and of commercial acts, but merely declared what was deducible from the legislation and jurisprudence in force and prevailing at the time it was promulgated.

It may probably therefore be safely assumed, that by an examination of the old law which is actually in force as law in Lower Canada, aided by the light which may be derived from the new law and from the commentators upon it, those transactions which are *Actes de Commerce*, can be accurately defined and ascertained, and that he may be taken to be a trader who engages in them and makes of them his habitual occupation.

The qualifying word " habitual," must not, however, be taken in a sense, either too wide or too narrow ; as always requiring a constant succession of commercial transactions, or as being always satisfied by the occurrence of a limited number of them. On the one hand a manifest intention to make of commerce a habitual occupation, will constitute a trader— though the acts of commerce really performed are few and infrequent. For instance the opening of a shop for the sale of goods—or of any particular kind of merchandise will qualify him who opens it, as a trader, though his actual sales may be few, or even though he may have failed to effect one. 2 Massé, p. 162,—1 Pardessus, p. 78,—1 Boulay-Paty, Des faillites, pp. 9, 10, 11. On the other hand a man may do commercial acts without thereby constituting himself a trader—for he may buy double the quantity of provision he requires for his household, with the intention of making a profit by the sale of what he does not want—and may actually sell and make that profit—yet he will not thereby become a trader. 1 Pard. loc. cit.,—1 Massé, p. 161,—Orillard, p. 4,—Bonnin, Leg. Com., p. 5. See also on these points, 1 Toub. vol. 1, pp. 274 et seq., though he strains the law in favor of the consular jurisdictions.

The English law on this point is in accordance with our own. There in order to make a man liable to be a bankrupt by buying or selling, or by the workmanship of goods or commodities, it was necessary that there should be a repeated practice of it, or a commencement of it, coupled with an intention to continue it ; for a single act of buying and selling, unaccompanied by such intention, would not be sufficient. But if that intention existed, the extent of the trading, whether large or trifling, would be immaterial. Archbold, p. 43, and cases cited. Wells vs. Parker, 11 T. Rep. 34, and Summersett vs. Jarvis, 3 Brod and Bing 2. In ex parte Magennis, 1 Rose 84, Lord Eldon said, " the question of trading depends not on the *quantum* of dealing, but the intention—and it is enough if a man will sell to any one who comes to buy." See also Ex parte Gallimore, 2 Rose 428— Holroyd, vs. Gwynne, 2 Taunt, 476.

To establish therefore that a man makes the engaging in commercial transactions his habitual occupation, evidence of the intent to do so, with but few instances in which he has done so, will suffice ; while if external evidence of the intent be wanting, a much more extensive series of transactions would be required to establish his commercial quality. And the Judge will be greatly facilitated in deciding upon such an enquiry, by the previous occupation of the man, his nominal occupation at the time, if he has any, and by the character of the transactions proved to have been entered into by him.

Taking then as guides to the interpretation of our Statute in the respect under consideration, the legislation and jurisprudence of France from the earliest times to the present day, the following persons may be suggested as being, amongst others, subject in Lower Canada to the provisions of our Statute :

1. Merchants, viz : persons habitually engaged in the buying and selling of goods, wares and merchandise for profit ;

2. Manufacturers of goods, wares or merchandise for sale ;

3. Bankers and dealers in money and commercial paper and securities ;

4. Factors or commission merchants ;

5. Brokers ;

6. Auctioneers ;

7. Insurers and underwriters ;

8. Common carriers for hire, whether by land or water ;

9. Hotel and tavern, eating-house and boarding-house keepers ;

10. Warehousemen and wharfingers ;

11. Mechanics and tradesmen who buy goods, wares or merchandise, either in the form of raw materials or wholly or partially manufactured, with intent to sell, after having by their labour improved the articles so purchased, or converted them into something else ; such as Jewellers— Boot and Shoemakers—Builders—Merchant tailors—Hatters and furriers— Watch and clockmakers— Shipbuilders—Printers—Butchers—Millers.

The proposition that mechanics and tradesmen under the circumstances mentioned, are traders, has been at times more or less disputed. Respectable jurisconsults of the sixteenth and seventeenth centuries are to be found who hold that he who purchased goods for the purpose of applying to them his own labor, and of afterwards selling them, was not a trader, although they admitted that he would be, if he so bought them with the view of causing them to be worked upon by others, and of afterwards selling them. See authors cited in 1 Massé, p. 20. And certain modern authors though unwilling to deny the general proposition, have endeavored to make a distinction between those artisans who buy materials and having worked upon them, offer them again for sale, and those who only buy such materials and bestow labour upon them when orders for them are received from a customer. The former they do not deny to be traders, but the latter they hesitate to admit into the rank of *Commerçants*, more especially if the work be of more value than the materials purchased. 1 Pardessus, No. 81. Armand Dalloz, Vo. Commerçant. § 20. But Mr. Pardessus in favoring a construction which seems to be founded on no principle, does so with such hesitation as to take from his opinions in this instance the weight which is ordinarily and justly attached to them. On the other side of the question, however, may be ranged a greater array of learned authors, who hold that the only distinction sustainable on principle is between the artisan who buys materials, and him who simply works at his trade. The first is a trader, the latter is not. 1 Toubeau, pp. 277, 278, 279. Jousse, Ord. de 1673. Tit. 12, art. 4. 5 Nouveau Denizart, p. 449. 1 Jur. Con. p. 17. 2

Bornier, 736. 1, Massé, pp. 20 et seq. 1 Boulay-Paty, Des faillites et Banq. p. 15. 1 Vincens, p. 126. Orillard, nos. 148, 149. 2 Carré, p. 542. And see also the numerous adjudged cases collected in De Villeneuve et Massé Dict. des Cont. Com. Vo. Commerçant, § 2.

In this respect the authorities upon the older English statutes, whose terms permit of no greater latitude of construction than those of the contemporaneous French enactments, are at one with the weight of authority in France. " Persons," says Mr. Eden, p. 8, " who buy the raw materials " of trade and sell them again under another form, or improved by the " labour of manufacture, have always been considered traders, liable to the " bankrupt laws, such as bakers, brewers, &c., who all purchase the raw " material, which they respectively manufacture and sell for a profit after " a certain amount of bodily labor has been expended upon it." See also the cases collected in Cooke, pp. 48 et seq. Daly vs. Smith, 4 Burr. 2148. 3 Mod. 330. Com. Dig. Bankrupt A.

In Lower Canada the laws respecting evidence in commercial cases and on the subject of trial by Jury, have rendered it occasionally necessary to discriminate between acts and persons possessing a commercial character and the contrary. The 25 Geo. III., cap. 2, already alluded to, provided that " every person having suits at law and actions in any of the said " Courts of Common Pleas grounded on debts, promises and contracts of a " mercantile nature only, between merchant and merchant, and trader and " trader, so reputed and understood according to law, should be entitled to " a trial by Jury." And although this restrictive provision has since been modified, (see the Statutes embodied in the Con. Stat. of L. C., pp. 791-2, and the Act of last session, intituled : " An Act respecting Juries and Jurors,") the character of the subject matter of the suit and of the parties engaged in it, has always been and still is an element in the consideration of the right to trial by Jury in civil matters.

And the same Ordinance, § 10, provided that " in proof of all facts con- " cerning commercial matters, recourse shall be had in all the Courts of " civil jurisdiction in this province, to the rules of evidence laid down by " the laws of England."

And again, the same Ordinance, § 38, authorized execution against the person of the defendant for the satisfaction of all judgments given in commercial matters between merchants and traders, as well as of all debts due to merchants or traders for goods, wares and merchandises by them sold.

And the Act 10 and 11 Vict., cap. 11, made various provisions respecting " Commercial matters", introducing with respect to actions based upon them, a particular species of limitation—and certain special rules of practice.

Upon these Statutes there have been frequent discussions in Lower Canadian Courts of justice, and although comparatively few of the decisions upon them have been preserved, owing to the want of reports while the jurisprudence was being settled—enough are to be found to indicate the views of our tribunals upon the points under consideration.

In Pozer vs. Meiklejohn, Pyke's Rep., p. 11, which was an action by a merchant against a brewer for the price of a quantity of beer stored with the latter, and not delivered back ; the English rules of evidence were held applicable.

In Pozer vs. Clapham, a demand for an alleged overpayment in making a return of the proceeds of goods sold at auction, was held to be a commercial matter. Stuart's Rep. 122.

In Patterson vs. Welsh, Quebec, 1819, a tavern keeper was held to be a trader. And a similar decision was rendered in McRoberts vs. Scott, Quebec, 1821.

In Rivers vs. Duncan, Quebec, 1819, it was held that in an action by a merchant against the master of a ship for the value of goods lost on a voyage to Quebec, the subject matter was between a merchant and a trader, and that either party had a right to a trial by jury.

Hiring river craft was held to be a fact of a commercial nature in Brehaut vs. Méran, Quebec, 1811.

The endorsement *pour aval* of a promissory note, is a fact concerning a commercial matter. Paterson vs. Pain, 1 L. C. Rep., p. 219.

The sale of a wagon and harness by a hotel keeper to the defendant described as *cultivateur et commerçant*, is a fact respecting a commercial matter. Vandal vs. Grenier, 6 L. C. Rep. 475.

A contract by a carpenter and joiner to build a house for a person not a trader, is a commercial matter. Kennedy vs. Smith, 6 L. C. Rep. p. 260.

A contract between a bricklayer and mason and a railway builder, is a commercial matter, as being one which in France would have been within the *jurisdiction consulaire*. Fahey vs. Jackson, 7 L. C., 27.

A contract of Insurance against fire between an insurance company and a non-trader, is a commercial matter. McGillivray vs. The Montreal Insurance Co. 8 L. C. Rep., p 401.

A contract to furnish materials for a house, and to build it, is a commercial contract. McGrath vs. Lloyd, 1 L. C. Jur., 17.

A contract of affreightment, is a commercial contract. The Secretary of State vs. Edmonstone et al., 6 L. C. Jur., p. 322.

A contract entered into with commissioners appointed under an Act of Parliament to provide stone for making a canal, is a commercial matter. Mackay and Ritherford, 13 Jur., 21.

On the other hand, a sale by the proprietor of a farm, to his lessee, of a quantity of firewood and hay remaining upon it when leased, is not a commercial transaction. Desbarats vs. Murray, 3 L. C. Jur., p. 27.

And a loan of money by a non-trader to a trader without averment that it referred to a commercial matter, is not a commercial fact. Wishaw vs. Gilmor, 6 L. C. Jur., 319.

A loan of money by a " bourgeois " to an " ouvrier " is not a commercial matter. Asselin vs. Mongeau, 5 L. C. Jur., 26.

OF VOLUNTARY ASSIGNMENTS.

<table>
<tr><td>Proceedings for voluntary assignment of an Insolvent estate ; meeting of creditors to be called.</td><td>2. Any person unable to meet his engagements, and desirous of making an assignment of his estate, or who is required so to do as hereinafter provided, may call a meeting of his creditors at his usual place of business, or at his option at any other place which may be more convenient for them ; and such meeting shall be called by advertisement (Form A), stating in such advertisement the object of such meeting ; and at such meeting he shall exhibit statements showing the position</td></tr>
<tr><td>Schedules of creditors, &c.</td><td>of his affairs, and particularly a schedule (Form B), containing the names and residences of all his creditors, and the amount due to each, distinguishing between those amounts which are actually overdue, or for which he is directly liable, and those for which he is only liable indirectly as endorser, surety or otherwise, and which have not become due at the date of such meeting ; and also the particulars of any nego-</td></tr>
<tr><td>Attestation.</td><td>tiable paper bearing his name, the holders of which are unknown to him,—which schedule shall be sworn to by the Insolvent, and may be corrected by him likewise under oath at the meeting at which it is so produced, also the amount due to each creditor, and a statement showing the amount and nature</td></tr>
<tr><td>Assets, books, &c.</td><td>of all his assets ; and he shall also produce his books of account, and all other documents and vouchers, if required so to do by any creditor :</td></tr>
</table>

1. *Or who is required so to do —*
Viz : by two or more creditors for sums exceeding in the aggregate $500. § 3, p. 2.

2. At his option at any other place—
There is no expressed restriction even as to the section of the Province in which the place of meeting may be fixed, provided it be more convenient to the creditors than the locality of the debtor's place of business. Thus the insolvent, being a resident of Montreal, might hold his preliminary meeting at Toronto, if the majority of his creditors resided at or near the latter city. But in such a case, care must be taken that an Assignee is appointed who is competent to act. If the creditors decide upon an Assignee, there would appear to be no obligation upon them to select one who resides within the County or District in which the insolvent's place of business is situate. But if the debtor is obliged to choose an Assignee from among the official assignees, he must select one who is resident within the same County or District as that in which he carries on his business, § 2, p. 4, § 3, p. 10, § 4, p. 1.
If the insolvent should either by error, or designedly, select a place of meeting, other than his place of business, and less convenient to his creditors, and assign to the assignee named at such meeting, his estate would become liable to compulsory liquidation under § 3, p. i. For this would not be a mere neglect or irregularity covered by p. 5 of § 2; but an assignment made "otherwise than in the manner prescribed by this Act."

3. By advertisement—
The mode of giving notice in all cases in which the act requires it to be given "by advertisement," is regulated by § 11, p. 1, which should be strictly followed.

4. Statements shewing the position of his affairs—
Ord. de 1673, tit. XI, art. 11. C. Com. art. 439. S. act § 81. E. act § 142.

5. Amounts which are actually overdue, or for which he is directly liable, and those for which he is only liable in directly, and which have not become due —
This distinction is required to enable the voting at the preliminary meeting to be properly regulated; those persons to whom the insolvent is directly liable, and those holding his overdue indirect liabilities being alone allowed to vote. Those holding immature claims upon which he is only liable indirectly as endorser, surety, or the like, are not allowed to vote, (p. 3, *post.*) Thus a holder of a bill not yet due, drawn or endorsed by the insolvent, would have no right to vote; but if the bill were dishonored before the meeting he could vote upon it. The object would seem to be to obtain the sense of those creditors really interested in the estate, which a person would not be merely because he held a bill or note, the acceptor or maker of which was solvent.

6. Particulars of negotiable paper bearing his name, the holders of which are unknown to him—
This is necessary in the interest of the creditors; but it also has an important bearing on the discharge of the insolvent. For if this class of paper be omitted from the Schedule, unless the unknown holder files his claim, the discharge does not relieve the insolvent from the debt due such holder. § 9, p. 3.

7. Sworn to—
In Lower Canada, before any Justice of the Peace or any Commissioner of the Superior Court. Con. Stat. L. C., p. 698.

2. Each notice of such meeting sent by post, as hereinafter provided, shall be accompanied by a list containing the names of all the creditors of the Insolvent whose claims exceed one hundred dollars, and the aggregate amount of those under one hundred dollars; *Notice by post.*

1. Sent by post—
When notice is required to be given "by advertisement," the person giving it, in addition to inserting it in newspapers, must also address and send by post, a similar notice to each interested party. § 11, p. 1.

2. *Whose claims exceed one hundred dollars—*
This paragraph speaks of claims *exceeding* $100, and of those *under* $100, but omits mention of such as amount exactly to $100. On the other hand the form of notice prescribed for use in the fulfilment of this provision, (Form A) describes the first class of claims as being *"for* one hundred dollars and upwards." The list should be made in conformity with the form.

The general rule as to voting gives the right of decision to the majority in number and value of the creditors present or represented, " for sums *above* one hundred dollars." § 11, p. 2.

The proportion in number of the creditors who may effectually discharge the debtor is described as the majority in number " for sums *of* one hundred dollars and upwards." § 9, p. 1.

And the same proportion of creditors may grant an allowance to the insolvent. § 5, p. 8.

It is probable that the distinction thus created was not contemplated in framing the Act, but care must be taken not to confound the two modes of computation.

Assignee appointed by creditors.
Votes of creditors.

Assignment.

3. At such meeting, the creditors may name an assignee, to whom such assignment may be made ; and if a vote be taken upon such nomination, each creditor shall only represent in such vote the amount of direct liabilities of the Insolvent to him, and the amount of indirect liabilities then actually overdue ; and thereafter the Insolvent shall make an assignment of his estate and effects to the assignee so chosen ;

1. *At such meeting—*
The meeting should be regularly organized. And correct minutes containing a list of all the creditors present or represented, and full details of all the proceedings, should be made at the time and preserved, in order that evidence of proceedings of such meeting may be available if subsequently required. And it would be proper to appoint a Chairman and Secretary as is usual at ordinary meetings. See Murdoch on Bankruptcy, p. 289, *in notis.*

2. *May name an Assignee—*
There is no restriction as to the person who may be nominated for Assignee by the creditors. He need not be a creditor, nor an official assignee.

3. *If a vote be taken—*
The majority in number of the creditors for sums above $100, present or represented will decide, if they also represent the majority in value, § 11, p. 2. If the two majorities differ—see *Ibid*, for the proceedings to be taken. In England the majority in value appoint, 24 and 25 V. 134, § 116. So also in Scotland, S. act § 181.

The mode of voting upon the nomination of an assignee, at the preliminary meeting, is not to be confounded with that to be adopted at the same meeting, upon incidental disputes as to the amount of a creditor's claim, and the like. The precautions taken for ascertaining and regulating the amount which each creditor may represent, render this plain. For instance, p. 1, not only requires that a statement of liabilities shewing the amount due to each creditor should be produced at this meeting, but also that the liabilities should be divided into two classes—direct, and overdue indirect— and indirect which are not due. And each creditor can only represent " the amount " of his direct and overdue indirect claims. P. 5, also provides that any dispute which arises as to the "amount " which any one of the creditors is entitled to represent in the nomination of an assignee, shall be disposed of by the votes of the majority in number. It is therefore clear, as already stated, that at this, as at all other meetings of creditors, the sense of the meeting is taken by a computation of value as well as number—according to the rule laid down in § 11, p. 2. The exceptions as to disputes about the amounts of claims, and other questions (which should probably be held to mean other *similar* questions) are made for convenience, as at the time of the first meeting no regular scrutiny of the claims can have been effected, or can be obtained.

4. *Thereafter—*

The time within which the assignment must be made is not limited by this clause, the debtor being allowed a certain discretionary latitude in the proceedings he voluntarily commences. But if any delay which occurs be such an unreasonable delay as to constitute a " neglect to proceed," the estate of the debtor becomes liable to compulsory liquidation,—§ 3, p. 4. And if such delay were to be accompanied by suspicious circumstances, such as continuance of trade, realization of assets, and the like, these would constitute other grounds for compulsory proceedings, under § 3, p. b and c.

4. If no assignee be named at such meeting, or at any adjournment thereof, or if the assignee named refuses to act, or if no creditor attends at such meeting, the Insolvent may assign his estate to any solvent creditor resident within this Province, not related, allied, or of kin to him, and being such creditor for a sum exceeding five hundred dollars, or if he has no such creditor for so large a sum who will accept such assignment, then to the creditor otherwise competent and willing to accept, representing the largest claim upon him ; or he may make such assignment to any official assignee resident within the district or county within which the Insolvent has his place of business and nominated for the purpose of this Act by the Board of Trade in such district or county, or if there be no Board of Trade therein, then by the nearest Board of Trade thereto ;

If no assignee be appointed by creditors, insolvent may select one.

Or assign to an Official assignee.

1. *To the creditor otherwise competent and willing to accept, representing the largest claim upon him—*

It might be contended that this clause means that among the creditors otherwise competent and willing to accept the office, he who holds the largest claim shall be selected as Assignee ; or that it provides that the insolvent is permitted to assign only to the largest claimant under $500, and if he be incompetent or unwilling to act, then that one of the official assignees must be selected. The first construction would seem to be most in accordance with the context, and with the spirit of the Act.

5. If any dispute arises at the first meeting of creditors as to the amount which any one of the creditors is entitled to represent in the nomination of an assignee, or upon any other question which may properly be discussed at such meeting, such dispute shall be decided by the votes of the majority in number of the creditors present, or represented by agents or proxies ; but if the dispute have reference to any pretension of any creditor as to the existence or amount of his claim, such creditor shall not vote upon the question ; but no neglect or irregularity in any of the proceedings antecedent to the appointment of the assignee shall vitiate an assignment subsequently made to an assignee competent to receive it under this Act ;

In case of dispute at first meeting of creditors, as to votes.

Irregularity not to vitiate appointment.

1. *If any dispute arises—*
See note 3 to § 2, p. 3.
2. *No neglect or irregularity —*
This provision appears to be intended to prevent the grave evil which would result to all parties concerned, if mere irregularities in proceedings antecedent to an assignment would avoid such assignment. The entire inob-

servance of any proceeding provided for by the act, would probably render the estate of the debtor liable to compulsory liquidation under § 3, p. i. But a defective performance of the requirements of the act in respect of any proceeding, would be cured, under this clause, by a subsequent assignment to a competent assignee. Voir Stat 1865 Sel. § 2

Form of Deed of assignment, &c.

Counterparts of deed.

6. The deed or instrument of assignment may be in the form C., or in any other form equivalent thereto, and if executed in Upper Canada shall be in duplicate; and a copy of the list of creditors produced at the first meeting of creditors shall be appended to it; and no particular description or detail of the property or effects assigned need be inserted in such deed; and any number of counterparts of such deed required by the assignee shall be executed by the Insolvent at the request of the assignee, either at the time of the execution of such deed or instrument, or afterwards, to which counterparts no list of creditors need be appended;

1. *No particular description or detail—*
There is nothing in the Act which requires that a debtor should have anything to assign; as in affording means of relief to debtors with insufficient assets, those who have none at all could not reasonably be excluded.
2. *Counterparts—*
For registration.

Effect of assignment, as to estate of insolvent.

Exception.

7. The assignment shall be held to convey and vest in the assignee, the books of account of the Insolvent, all vouchers, accounts, letters and other papers and documents relating to his business, all moneys and negotiable paper, stocks, bonds, and other securities, as well as all the real estate of the Insolvent, and all his interest therein, whether in fee or otherwise, and also all his personal estate, and moveable and immoveable property, debts, assets and effects, which he has or may become entitled to at any time before his discharge is effected under this Act, excepting only such as are exempt from seizure and sale under execution, by virtue of the several statutes in such case made and provided;

1. *Excepting only such as are exempt—*
See Cons. Stat. L. C., pp. 795-6. E. act. § 117.

Duplicate or authentic copy of assignment to be deposited, and where.

8. Forthwith upon the execution of the deed of assignment, the assignee, if appointed in Upper Canada, shall deposit one of the duplicates thereof, and if in Lower Canada, an authentic copy thereof, in the office of the proper Court; and in either case the said list of creditors shall accompany the deed or instrument so deposited;

1. *The proper Court—*
That is, in Upper Canada, in the office of the County Court, in the County or Union of Counties in which the proceedings are carried on. And in Lower Canada, in the office of the Prothonotary of the Superior Court in the District in which the proceedings are carried on. § 12, p. 4.

9. If the Insolvent possesses real estate, the deed of assignment may be enregistered in the Registry Office for the Registration Division or County within which such real estate is situate ; and no subsequent registration of any deed or instrument of any kind executed by the Insolvent, or which otherwise would have affected his real estate, shall have any force or effect thereon ; and if the real estate be in Upper Canada and the deed of assignment be executed in Lower Canada before Notaries, a copy of the deed certified under the hand and official seal of the Notary or other public officer in whose custody the original remains, may be registered without other evidence of the execution thereof, and without any memorial ; and a certificate of such registration may be endorsed upon a like copy ; and if the property be in Lower Canada and the deed of assignment be executed in Upper Canada, it may be enregistered by memorial or at full length in the usual manner ; but it shall not be necessary to enregister, or to refer on registration in any manner to the list of creditors annexed to the deed of assignment ;

Registration of deed of assignment, if the insolvent has real estate.

Assignment executed in L. C. or U. C. how registered in the other section of the Province.

10. If such deed be executed in Upper Canada, according to the form of execution of deeds prevailing there, it shall have the same force and effect in Lower Canada as if it had been executed in Lower Canada before notaries ; and if such deed be executed in Lower Canada before notaries it shall have the same force and effect in Upper Canada, as if it had been executed in Upper Canada, according to the law in force there ; and copies of such deed, certified as aforesaid, shall constitute, before all courts and for all purposes, *primâ facie* proof of the execution and of the contents of the original of such deed without production of the original.

Deed executed in U. C. form to have force in L. C. and vice versâ.

If Notarial.

COMPULSORY LIQUIDATION.

3. A debtor shall be deemed insolvent and his estate shall become subject to compulsory liquidation :

In what cases the estate of an insolvent trader shall become subject to compulsory liquidation.

Insolvent—
Persons unable to meet their liabilities, have been divided into two or more classes both in England and France—the distinction between them having relation either to their occupations, or to their conduct.

In England the broad distinction between an insolvent and a Bankrupt was that the latter was a trader, while the former generally was not. The degree of the relief to which these classes were respectively entitled was different also, the Bankrupt being as a rule capable of obtaining a discharge from his debts, while the insolvent could only receive protection from process. In consequence of these distinctions the words Bankrupt and Insolvent had a precise technical signification, and conveyed very different ideas, although the laws applicable to both differed only in detail, except as to the relief which the debtor could obtain for himself. The Bankruptcy Act of 1861, seems however to have abolished the insolvent courts, and to have made every one amenable to a system to which the term Bankruptcy is applied. The word "insolvent" therefore is not used in this Act in the sense it had acquired in England, but corresponds with the English word Bankrupt in its more modern meaning.

In France the inability of a person to meet his engagements might be described as *déconfiture*, or as *faillite*, and the *faillite* under certain circumstances became *banqueroute*.

A state of *déconfiture*—which is synonimous with *insolvabilité* (Nouv. Den. Vo. Déconfiture) is described, by the law of Lower Canada, as existing "quand les biens du débiteur, tant meubles qu'immeubles, ne suffisent " aux créanciers apparents." (Cout. de Paris, Art. 180.)

But in France, the mere stoppage of payment by a trader causes *faillite*.— And the question whether his assets if realised, would meet his engagements or not, is of no importance. " La faillite est un état de cessation de paiemens, ou pour cause d'insolvabilité réelle ou pour cause d'embarras dans les affaires." Celui qui cesse ces paiemens dans le langage de commerce (says Boulay-Paty)—est en état de faillite pour ses créanciers. Peu importe que d'ailleurs il puisse être solvable : sitôt qu'il n'acquitte plus ses obligations commerciales il faillit à ses engagements, et sa conduite, comme commerçant doit être examinée." Boulay-Paty, Tit. 1, Sec. 1.

But the word Bankruptcy,—*banqueroute*,—under the French system, still conveys the meaning which it originally possessed in England—namely, that the misfortune of the debtor is not unaccompanied by a greater or less degree of culpability. " La Banqueroute est l'état de tout commerçant failli contre lequel s'élèvent des faits d'inconduite, d'imprudence ou de fraude." 3. Bedarride, No. 1202. Nouv. Den. Vo. Banqueroute ; Jousse, Ord. 1673, p. 149.

But while these or similar distinctions have prevailed in France for several centuries, and are familiar to every lawyer, they are not recognized as law in Lower Canada. Any person, whether a trader or non-trader, may fall into a state of *déconfiture*, or actual and absolute insolvability : but the stoppage of payment has no legal effect, except as a circumstance which may create a presumption of the insufficiency of a debtor's assets, and thereby aid in establishing his insolvability.

In the present Act the words " insolvent " and " insolvency " are used in a similar sense to the words " Bankrupt " and " Bankruptcy " in England, and to the words "*failli* " and "*faillite* " in France. It is not necessary that a debtor should be actually *en déconfiture*, to bring him within the purview of the Act. It is sufficient if by any of the acts or defaults specified in the law, he satisfies its conditions : and except in one particular case, (§ 3, p. 3,) the question whether or no his assets will finally pay his debts in full or not, is not material. But under this Act, as in England, no distinction exists between what would be called in France *faillite* and *banqueroute*, except in so far as the facts constituting the latter state, may operate to prevent the insolvent from obtaining his discharge, or retard him in so doing.

<table>
<tr><td>Debtor abs-
conding.</td><td>*a.* If he absconds or is immediately about to abscond from this Province with intent to defraud any creditor, or to defeat or delay the remedy of any creditor, or to avoid being arrested or served with legal process, or if being out of the Province he so remains with a like intent, or if he conceals himself within this Province with a like intent ;</td></tr>
</table>

a. Absconds, or is immediately about to abscond, with intent to defraud—
These have long been sufficient grounds in Lower Canada for the issue of a *capias ad respondendum*, or of a *saisie-arrêt* before judgment ; to the latter of which processes the writ of attachment under this Act is assimilated. The jurisprudence already established as to the construction of these provisions, the nature of the evidence which will be held to establish the intention to abscond, &c., will therefore be of service to the practitioner in acting upon this clause.

See Ross vs. Burns, 7 L. C. Jur., p. 35. Lamarche vs. Lebrocq, 1 L. C., p. 215. Benjamin vs. Wilson, 1 L. C., 351. Leeming vs. Cochrane, *ibid*, p. 352. Cornell vs. Merritt, *ibid*, p. 357. Wilson vs. Reid, 4 L. C., p. 157.

Wilson vs. Ray, *ibid*, p. 159. Berry vs. Dixon, *ibid*, p. 218. Larocque vs. Clarke, *ibid*, p. 402. Hasset vs. Mulcahay, 6 L. C., p. 15. Talbot vs. Donnelly, 11 L. C., p. 5 Tremaine vs. Sansouci, 4 L. C. Jur., p. 148. McDougall vs. Torrance, 4 L. C. Jur., p. 148. Dumont vs. Court, *ibid*, p. 119.

The English Bankruptcy law has a very similar provision in the 12, 13 Vict. c. 106, § 67, which is not repealed by the new statute ; and this clause in its turn was taken nearly *verbatim* from the 6 Geo. 4, cap. 16, § 3. And a similar enactment is made in § 70, of the Bankruptcy Act of 1861, as to non-traders. An immense mass of authorities on the construction of this and the other definitions of acts of Bankruptcy contained in those sections, is collected in 1 Doria and Macrae, on Bankruptcy, pp. 127 et seq. ; also, in Archbold, on Bankruptcy, pp. 48, 49, 62, 63, and in Griffith's Bankruptcy Act, pp. 31 et seq.

b. Or if he secretes or is immediately about to secrete any part of his estate and effects with intent to defraud his creditors or to defeat or delay their demands or any of them ; **Secreting estate.**

*Or if he secretes, or is immediately about to secrete, * * * with intent, &c.*

This also under the existing law of Lower Canada, forms a sufficient ground for the issue of a *cap. ad res.* or of a *saisie arrêt* before judgment. And there are numerous cases reported, illustrative of the construction put upon this provision by the Courts.

See Shaw vs. McConnell, 4 L. C., 49. Dumont vs. Court, 7 L. C. Jur., 119. Molson's Bank vs. Leslie, Montreal, 1863. Macfarlane vs. Lynch, Montreal, 1864. Langley vs. Chamberlin, 5 L. C. Jur., 49.

There does not appear to be any act of Bankruptcy similarly described in the English Acts, though some of those which are to be found there, might constitute a fraudulent secreting. Such, for instance, as the Bankrupt making a fraudulent grant, conveyance, gift, delivery or transfer of his assets, which was the act that was held to be a fraudulent secreting in Langley vs. Chamberlin, and in Molson's Bank vs. Leslie.

c. Or if he assigns, removes or disposes of, or is about or attempts to assign, remove or dispose of any of his property with intent to defraud, defeat or delay his creditors or any of them ; **Fraudulently assigning.**

Or if he assigns, removes or disposes of, with intent, &c.

This would seem to be very similar in its purport to the last clause, at least as regards Lower Canada. The acts described in it would constitute a fraudulent secreting. It is nearly identical with the acts of Bankruptcy, twelfthly and fourteenthly mentioned in the English Act, and would be construed in Upper Canada in a similar manner. See the discussion of these clauses and the cases collected upon them, in Archbold on Bankruptcy, pp. 51 et seq., and 1 Doria vs. Macrae, on Bankruptcy, pp. 136 et seq.

d. Or if with such intent he has procured his money, goods, chattels, lands or property to be seized, levied on or taken under or by any process or execution, having operation where the debtor resides or has property, founded upon a demand in its nature provable under this Act and for a sum exceeding two hundred dollars, and if such process is in force and not discharged by payment or in any manner provided for by law ; **Or procuring it to be seized in execution.**

Or if with such intent he has procured his money, goods, &c., to be taken in execution.
See 10th Act of Bankruptcy in English Act. Archbold, p. 54. 1 Doria and M., p. 134.

Or being imprisoned in civil action.

e. Or if he has been actually imprisoned or upon the gaol limits for more than thirty days in a civil action founded on contract for the sum of two hundred dollars or upwards, and still is so imprisoned or on the limits ; or if in case of such imprisonment he has escaped out of prison or from custody or from the limits ;

Or if he has been actually imprisoned.
A similar provision to this is to be found in § 71 of the English Bankruptcy Act of 1861, which is however merely a re-enactment of a clause of the English Act, of 1849, (§ 69). See Archbold, p 63, and 1 Doria and Macrae, p. 156.

Or refusing to appear.

f. Or if he wilfully neglects or refuses to appear on any rule or order requiring his appearance to be examined as to his debts under any statute or law in that behalf ;

Or to obey orders for payment.

g. Or if he wilfully refuses or neglects to obey or comply with any such rule or order made for payment of his debts or of any part of them ;

Or any order or decree in Chancery.

h. Or if he wilfully neglects or refuses to obey or comply with the order or decree of the Court of Chancery or of any of the judges thereof, for payment of money ;

Or if he wilfully refuses or neglects to obey an order to appear for examination ;
Or to pay his debts ;
Or to pay money.
These are similar to the 76th and following sections of the English Act of 1861, and they are more particularly applicable to Upper Canada.

Or assigning generally, except under this Act.

i. Or if he has made any general conveyance or assignment of his property for the benefit of his creditors, otherwise than in the manner prescribed by this Act :

Or if he has made any general conveyance or assignment.
This would be held in England to be an act of Bankruptcy, as being of necessity a fraudulent conveyance, because it is said, as the result would be to defeat or delay the creditors, such would be held to be the intent. Stewart vs. Moody, 1 Scott, 777. Siebert vs. Spooner, 1 M. and W. 714. Chase vs. Goble, 3 Scott N. R., 245. By making it a substantive act of Bankruptcy, however, its application is extended, and discussion is prevented.

Demand of assignment, if trader does not meet his commercial liabilities.

2. If a trader ceases to meet his commercial liabilities generally as they become due, any two or more creditors for sums exceeding in the aggregate five hundred dollars, may make a demand upon him (Form E.) requiring him to make an assignment of his estate and effects for the benefit of his creditors ;

1. *If a trader ceases to meet his commercial liabilities generally as they become due —*

The stoppage of payment by a trader has always been regarded in the commercial world as an indication if not as conclusive proof of insolvency. If not proof of the insufficiency of the debtors assets, it establishes his inability to carry on his business ; or in other words to fulfil his engagements to his creditors. Whenever this occurs it becomes the right of the creditors to enquire into the affairs of their debtor, and his duty fu'ly to inform them of everything which it is their interest to know. All this would result from natural equity as applied to the relations between the debtor and his creditors ; and practically obtains whenever the failing debtor is disposed to deal fairly with his creditors. And it is at this point that it becomes also the interest of the creditors to assume an active part in the management of the debtor's estate ;—for the fact of his cessation of payments affords a strong probability, and as experience has shewn, almost a certainty, that his assets will do no more than pay them what is due There has been great diversity of opinion on the question whether or no, the power of assuming possession of the estate should be given to the creditors at this stage, and the legislation of the two great commercial countries of Europe has been dissimilar on this point.

In England the entire stoppage of payment by a debtor would not render him amenable to the Bankrupt law, the acts of Bankruptcy there being divisible into two leading classes, acts of the Bankrupt tending to defraud his creditors or impede their remedies against him ; and neglects of the Bankrupt to obey judgments or orders of some Court.

In France on the other hand the stoppage of payment has long been regarded as a ground for transferring the administration of the debtor's estate from himself to some person representing his creditors.

Although this is not declared in the Ord. of 1673 to be an indication of *faillite*, yet, says M. Jousse, p. 150 : *La faillite ou banqueroute est aussi réputée ouverte du jour que le débiteur est devenu insolvable, et a cessé entièrement de payer ses créanciers.*

In the Code de Commerce of 1807, and in the amendments of 1838, the stoppage of payment is declared to constitute a state of insolvency. *Tout commerçant qui cesse ses paiemens est en état de faillite.* Art. 437.

The present act has adopted a middle course between these two extremes, and without either denying a reasonable weight or presumption of insolvency to the stoppage of payment, or treating it as the inclusive presumption ; enables the creditors upon its occurrence to set the machinery of the act in motion towards procuring the control of the estate. If the debtor should prove to be really insolvent ; and as will be seen hereafter provides a means of arresting the proceedings, if the stoppage is fortuitous and temporary.

The words of the act seem to constitute merely an expansion or explanation of the usual phrase applicable to such a state of things stoppage of payments—*cessation de paiemens.* And they embody in a few words the interpretation given to the 437th article of the Code de Commerce by writers of authority. The phrase "ceases to meet his engagements generally as they become due," would not usually be satisfied by one or even several protests of negotiable paper, if the debtor continued his business and manifested in no other way any disorder in his affairs. M. Pardessus remarks upon this point with his usual practical sense —*on ne devrait pas toujours voir un signe de cessation de paiemens dans un ou quelques protêts. Combien de commerçans, même dans les grandes villes, mais surtout dans les petites, où les ressources pour réaliser promptement, soit des effets à longs termes soit des marchandises, sont extrêmement rares, se trouvent avoir leurs magasins et leur portefeuilles remplis et sont néanmoins forcés de laisser protester des engagemens qu'ils acquittent ensuite !* 4 Pard. p. 258, No. 1101. See also 1 Bedarride. des Faillites No. 18. 2 Massé, 1148. *De même* (says M. Renouard, p 127) *que quelques paiemens refusés, pour des motifs spéciaux, ou par suite de contestations particulières, ne constituent pas en faillite le commerçant qui continue à acquitter régulièrement l'ensemble de ses engagemens ; de même aussi quelques paiemens opérés n'empêchent pas que la faillite ait lieu.* La discrétion of the Judge

2*

or Court must be exercised in the decision of each case according to circumstances, for it is plain that the same number of failures to pay, which in one case would be disregarded as affording no evidence of stoppage, might in another establish it conclusively. The words of the clause would seem to avoid ambiguity as much as could be anticipated. Payments of commercial liabilities generally must cease, which could not be said of isolated and intermittent instances of non payment. While it might with propriety be considered to have taken place, though but few cases of non payment had occurred, where the debts left unpaid were large, and where payment was not resumed.

It is also made essential that the unpaid liabilities should be commercial, thus constituting the only case in which the jurisdiction created by the act is both real and personal. This is similar to the rule of the French law, as expressly enacted in the Code of 1807, art. 441 ; and as established by the opinions of the writers upon the amendment of 1838. 2 Massé, p. 307. 1 Bedarride, des faillites, p. 27.

2. *Any two or more creditors—*

An additional precaution against a misconstruction of this clause, and against the use of the act by an exacting creditor as a mode of enforcing payment of a debt.

3. *May make a demand upon him—*

The demand should be in duplicate, and one duplicate should be preserved, with a note by the person who served it upon the debtor, of the time and place of service.

<table>
<tr><td>Counter petition denying the truth of the allegations in such demand.</td><td>3. If the trader on whom such demand is made, contends that the claims of such creditors do not together amount to five hundred dollars, or that they were procured in whole or in part for the purpose of enabling such creditors to take proceedings under this Act ; or that the stoppage of payment by such trader was only temporary, and that it was not caused by any fraud or fraudulent intent, or by the insufficiency of the assets of such trader to meet his liabilities, he may, within five days from such demand, present a petition to the judge praying that no further proceedings under this Act may be taken upon such</td></tr>
</table>

Counter petition denying the truth of the allegations in such demand.

3. If the trader on whom such demand is made, contends that the claims of such creditors do not together amount to five hundred dollars, or that they were procured in whole or in part for the purpose of enabling such creditors to take proceedings under this Act ; or that the stoppage of payment by such trader was only temporary, and that it was not caused by any fraud or fraudulent intent, or by the insufficiency of the assets of such trader to meet his liabilities, he may, within five days from such demand, present a petition to the judge praying that no further proceedings under this Act may be taken upon such

Judge to decide.

demand ; and, after hearing the parties and such evidence as may be adduced before him, the judge may grant the prayer of his petition and thereafter such demand shall have no force or effect whatever ; and such petition may be granted with or without costs against either party ; but if it appears to the judge that such demand has been made without reasonable grounds, and merely as a means of enforcing payment under color of proceeding under this Act, he may condemn the creditors making it to pay treble costs ;

1 *Within five days—*

Juridical days. § 12, p. 5. Rules of practice, No. 12.

2. *Present a Petition—*

Of which notice should be given to the creditors signing the demand. And one clear day for each fifteen miles of distance between the place where the petition is to be presented and the residence of the party notified, or the place of service, will be sufficient. § 1, p. 9.

3. *To the Judge—*

In Upper Canada to the Judge of the County Court for the County or Union of Counties in which the demand is made. In Lower Canada to the Judge of the Superior Court having jurisdiction in the district within which the demand is made. § 12, p. 4. See also as to Lower Canada the Cons. Stat. for L. C., Cap. 78, § 24, 25.

4. *That the stoppage of payment was only temporary, and that it was not caused by fraud or insufficiency of assets —*

This provision is implied in the terms of p. 2, inasmuch as that p. requires that there should be a cessation of payment of liabilities generally, which condition would not be satisfied by a temporary and accidental stoppage occurring from other causes than from insolvency. The intention of the Legislature is thus placed beyond doubt, and the validity of the demand is made to depend upon the existence of a state of things incompatible with the successful prosecution of the debtor's business.

It must be observed however that the act does not make the temporary character of the stoppage alone, sufficient to relieve the debtor from the obligation sought to be imposed upon him by the demand. If his assets appear to be insufficient to meet his liabilities, and this insufficiency was the cause even of a temporary stoppage ; or if the stoppage was for a fraudulent purpose ; the proceeding is allowed to go on. And it seems in accordance with the objects of such a law that it should ; as in the one case actual insolvability is established, of which stoppage of payment is only one of the *indicia ;* and in the other, a state of things which under most systems of law justifies the deprivation of the debtor, of all control over his estate.

5. *Without reasonable grounds —*

This would seem to apply only to the three grounds mentioned in this clause, any one of which would be sufficient to sustain a petition for protection. But the context shows that the evil more particularly intended to be guarded against, was the converting the procedure indicated by the act into a mere collecting process, which could be used against any trader who omitted to pay a debt, instead of being used only against traders who were really insolvent.

4. If such petition be rejected ; or if while such petition is pending, the debtor continues his trade, or proceeds with the realization of his assets ; or if no such petition be presented within the aforesaid time, and the insolvent during the same time neglects to call a meeting of his creditors as provided by the second section of this Act ; or if he does not complete such assignment within three days after such meeting, or if there be an adjournment thereof, then within three days after such adjournment ; or if having given notice of a meeting of creditors, as required by the second section of this Act, he neglects to proceed further thereunder, his estate shall become subject to compulsory liquidation ; *If the petition be rejected or none be presented, &c.* *Liquidation to be compulsory.*

1. *If the Insolvent neglects to call a meeting —*

The 87th chapter of the Consolidated Statutes for Lower Canada enacts that somewhat similar facts shall constitute a sufficient ground for the issue of a *saisie-arrêt* before judgment, or a *capias ad respondendum.* It is therein enacted, that if it be stated in an affidavit that the defendant is a trader ; that he is notoriously insolvent ; that he has refused to compromise or arrange with his creditors, or to make a *cession de biens* to them, or for their benefit, and that he continues to carry on his trade, the debtor shall be held to be about to secrete his goods and chattels with intent to defraud his creditors. Cons. Stat. L. C., cap. 87, § 9.

5. But no act or omission shall justify any proceeding to place the estate of an insolvent in compulsory liquidation, unless proceedings are taken under this Act 'in respect of the same, within three months next after the act or omission relied upon as subjecting such estate thereto ; nor after a voluntary *But proceedings must be taken within three months.*

assignment has been made, or an assignee appointed under this Act ;

1. *Within three months—*
In England the period is twelve months. Consolidation Act of 1849, § 88. In Scotland four months ; Murdoch, 223.

2. *After a voluntary assignment has been made—*
That is, a voluntary assignment made in the manner prescribed by the Act ; for an assignment made in any other way would be of itself sufficient ground for proceedings in compulsory liquidation

Proceedings for issue of Writ of attachment of debtors estate, in L. C.

6. In Lower Canada an affidavit may be made by a creditor for a sum not less than two hundred dollars, or by the clerk or other duly authorized agent of such creditor, setting forth the particulars of his debt, the insolvency of the person indebted to him, and any fact or facts which, under this Act, subject the estate of such debtor to compulsory liquidation (Form F), and upon such affidavit being filed with the Prothonotary of the district within which the insolvent has his place of business, a writ of attachment (Form G) shall issue against the estate and effects of the insolvent addressed to the sheriff of the district in which such writ issues, requiring such sheriff to seize and attach the estate and effects of the insolvent, and to summon him to appear before the court to answer the premises, within such time as is usual therein for the return of ordinary writs of summons ; and such writ shall be accompanied by a declaration setting forth such facts and circumstances as are necessary to be proved to sustain the issue thereof; and shall be subject as nearly as can be to the rules of procedure of the court in ordinary suits, as to its issue, service, return and subsequent proceedings ;

Declaration to accompany writ.

.

1. *An affidavit—*
Sworn to before any Judge or Commissioner for taking affidavits in the Superior Court. The proceeding prescribed by this section is almost identical with that already prevailing in Lower Canada with regard to writs of *saisie-arrêt* before judgment and of *capias ad respondendum.* Rule 13.

2. *For a sum not less than two hundred dollars—*
This would seem to be sufficient, even in cases where proceedings have commenced by a demand of assignment which requires two creditors claiming not less than five hundred dollars. That Act of Insolvency once perfected, may therefore be taken advantage of by any creditor who could initiate proceedings upon the occurrence of any other.

3. *And shall be subject as nearly as can be to the rules of procedure—*
There is no provision in the law that would necessarily cause any departure from the ordinary rules of procedure of the Superior Court, until after the return of the writ. Then there is an entire change, as the mode in which the allegations essential to the support of the writ are assailed, is by petition, and not by exception or plea. Post, p. 12. But the proceeding upon the petition would then be conducted in conformity with the usual practice of the Court, as directed by this clause. And after such petition is disposed of, either by proceeding to the appointment of an assignee or by quashing the writ, no further step seems to be required in the case. The reason doubtless is, that no condemnation is sought against the insolvent by the proceeding, the only object being the maintenance of the writ ; and therefore the correctness of its issue is tested in the same way as that of a *capias*, the result being conclusive as to the whole proceeding, and rendering pleas unnecessary. Rules 15, 16, 19, 20,

7. In Upper Canada, in case any creditor by affidavit The same in
of himself or any other individual (Form F), shows to the U. C.
satisfaction of the judge that he is a creditor of the insolvent
for a sum of not less than two hundred dollars, and also
shews by the affidavits of two credible persons, such
facts and circumstances as satisfy such judge that the
debtor is insolvent within the meaning of this Act, and that
his estate has become subject to compulsory liquidation,
such judge may order the issue of a writ of attachment
(Form G) against the estate and effects of the insolvent,
addressed to the sheriff of the county in which such writ issues,
requiring such sheriff to seize and attach the estate and effects
of the insolvent and to summon him to appear before the court
to answer the premises, within such time as is usual therein
for the return of ordinary writs of summons ; and such writ Declaration
shall be accompanied by a declaration setting forth such facts to accompany
and circumstances as are necessary to be proved to maintain writ.
the issue thereof, and shall be subject as nearly as can be to
the rules of procedure of the Court in ordinary suits as to its
issue, return, and subsequent proceedings ;

In Upper Canada—
The procedure indicated by this clause, is intended to bear the same
relation to existing practice in Upper Canada as that prescribed by the last
previous clause does to the Lower Canadian system.

8. Immediately upon the issue of a writ of attachment under Notice of issue
this Act, the Sheriff shall give notice thereof by advertisement of writ.
thereof (Form H) ;

This notice is intended to prevent third parties from permitting, or partici-
pating in. any attempt to make away with the estate, or with any part of it
over which they may have control.

9. Under such writ of attachment the Sheriff shall, by himself How writ
or by such agent or messenger as he shall appoint for that pur- shall be exe-
pose, whose authority shall be established by a copy of the writ cuted.
addressed to him by name and description, and certified under
the hand of the Sheriff, seize and attach all the estate and
effects of the insolvent wherever situate, including his books of
account, moneys and securities for money, and all his office or
business papers, documents, and vouchers of every kind and
description ; and shall return, with the writ, a report under Return
oath of his action thereon ;

1. *Report under oath—*
This does not appear to contemplate the making of a detailed inventory
of the effects seized. for that is afterwards provided for, *post* p. 11. But
merely a report in general terms that he has performed the duty required of
him. See Rule 21.

10. If the Board of Trade in the County or District in which In whose cus-
is situate the place of business of the debtor, or if there be no tody property

attached shall be placed in L. C. Board of Trade in such County or District, then the Board of Trade nearest thereto, has appointed official assignees for the purposes of this Act, the Sheriff shall place the estate and effects attached in the custody of one of such official assignees, who shall be guardian under such writ ; but if not he shall appoint as guardian such solvent and responsible person as may be willing to assume such guardianship ;

Nearest thereto.   See note to § 4, p. 1, *post.*

Duty of such person.   11. The person so placed in possession shall forthwith proceed to make an inventory of the estate and effects of the defendant ; and also such statements of his affairs as can be **Inventory, &c.** made from the books, accounts and papers attached ; And he shall file such inventory in the Court on the return day of the writ ; and shall produce such statements at the meeting of creditors called for the appointment of an official assignee ;

1. *An Inventory—*
This is in lieu of the detailed inventory which would otherwise require to be made by the seizing officer. And it should be prepared with such accuracy and completeness, as to constitute a detailed description of the debtors estate, including his books of account and most important documents :—and should be authenticated by the person making it, in such a manner as to afford conclusive evidence against him afterwards, if he should fail to deliver any part of the estate to the assignee.
2. *Statements of his affairs—*
These should be similar statements to those which the insolvent is bound to produce at the preliminary meeting of his creditors. § 1, p. 1.
3. *He shall file such inventory* * * * *and shall produce such statements.*
These duties could be enforced by rule, and t eir neglect punished by *contrainte,* the guardian being an officer of the Court. But the non-performance of these duties at the time prescribed, would not affect the validity of the proceedings.

Petition to set aside attachment.   12. Except in cases where a petition has been presented as provided for by the third paragraph of this section, the alleged insolvent may present a petition to the Judge at any time within five days from the return day of the writ, but not afterwards, and may thereby pray for the setting aside of the attachment made under such writ, on the ground that his estate **To be decided summarily.** has not become subject to compulsory liquidation ; and such petition shall be heard and determined by the Judge in a summary manner, and conformably to the evidence adduced before him thereon ;

1. *Except in cases where a petition has been presented—*
This exception is inserted because the previous petition, if one was presented, must have substantially covered the same ground, as that permitted by this clause.
2. *May present a petition -*
This is evidently instead of a plea or exception. (See note to p. 6).
3. *Five days—*
Juridical days. § 12, p. 5. Rule No.
4. *That his estate has not become subject to compulsory liquidation—*
This is the substantive question which must be raised by the petition.

but the special grounds of defence to the allegations of the affidavit or of the declaration should be set forth in the petition, or those allegations denied. In other words as the alleged insolvent must rely either upon the falsehood of the statements of his opponent, or upon other facts which avoid their effect, or upon both, he must shew by his petition the position he assumes, just as he would do if the proceeding were an ordinary action, and he were pleading to it.

5. *Conformably to the evidence adduced—*
That is to say, adduced according to the same rules as to the right to begin, the burden of proof and the like, as in ordinary cases.

13. Immediately upon the expiration of five days from the return day of the writ, if no petition to quash or to stay proceedings be filed, or upon the rendering of judgment on the petition to quash, if it be dismissed, the Judge upon the application of the plaintiff, or of any creditor intervening for the prosecution of the cause, shall order a meeting of the creditors to be held before him or any other Judge, at a time and place named in such order, and after due notice thereof, for the purpose of giving their advice upon the appointment of an official assignee ; *Meeting of creditors for appointment of official assignee.*

1. *Immediately upon the expiration of five days —*
That is after five clear juridical days have expired exclusive of the day of the return and of the application. And this clause further confirms the view that no plea or exception can be filed, for the only contingencies which can prevent the order being given for the first meeting, are the presentation of a petition to quash, or to stay proceedings.

2. *Or to stay proceedings —*
Under p. 15, *post.*

3. *Or of any creditor intervening —*
When the machinery for compulsory liquidation has once been set in motion, any creditor may press on the procedure as well as the plaintiff. The debtor therefore has no temptation to enter into corrupt arrangements with the plaintiff, with a view to arresting the proceedings.

4. *And after due notice thereof—*
§ 11, p. 1, provides that notices of meetings of creditors shall be given by publication thereof for two weeks in the Canada Gazette, &c., and also that notices be sent by post to the creditors, by the " Assignee or person " calling such meeting. That provision would however seem inapplicable to this clause, as no list of creditors is attainable at this stage of the proceedings, and there is no " assignee or person " calling the meeting. To avoid difficulty therefore, the Judge's order for the meeting should declare what notice should be given, and that order should require at least the same number of advertisements as those provided for in § 11, p. 1.

5. *Giving their advice —*
This is the mode in which Tutors and Curators are appointed in Lower Canada. And in this case it will render unnecessary any preliminary enquiry into the amounts actually due to creditors, leaving that matter to be subsequently developed under the scrutiny of the assignee. The present French law adopts a similar mode of election : the opinions only of the creditors being taken by the Juge-Commissaire, and the appointment being made by the Court. C. Com. art. 462. See the remarks of M. Bedarride on this provision, which are in a great degree applicable to this clause of the Statute, Vol. 1, p. 295.

6. *Official Assignee —*
So called with reference to the mode of appointment, to distinguish it from the appointment of an assignee by a voluntary deed of assignment. But there is no difference in the powers or duties of the assignees in whichever mode they may be invested with the office.

Who may be appointed official assignee.

14. At the time and place appointed, and on hearing the advice of the creditors present upon oath (Form I,) the Judge shall appoint some person to be such official assignee, which person shall be the person proposed by the creditors present, if they are unanimous ; and if they are not unanimous, then the judge may appoint either one of the persons proposed by the creditors, or one of the official assignees named by the Board of Trade ;

If they are unanimous —
The Judge has no discretionary power in the appointment of an assignee, if the creditors agree. If they differ, the power immediately becomes vested solely in him, but his choice is restricted to the persons proposed by the creditors, and to those named by the Board of Trade, for Official Assignees. The reasons given by the creditors for their advocacy of one candidate, or opposition to another, will probably render it easy to avoid appointing an unfit person. And in case of doubt, an assignee may advantageously be selected from the list of official assignees, deposited by the Board of Trade with the Prothonotary or Clerk. § 4, p. 1. One of whom will probably be then in possession of the estate as guardian. *Ante.* p. 10.

Debtor may petition for suspension of proceedings.

15. Instead of petitioning to quash the attachment, the debtor may, within the like delay, petition the judge to suspend further proceedings against·him, and to that end to submit such petition to a meeting of the creditors and the debtor to be called for that purpose, in order that the creditors may determine whether the proceedings against the debtor shall be suspended or not ;

1. *Instead of petitioning to quash —*
This, and the next seven sections provide a mode by which an estate which may be more advantageously wound up by the debtor himself, and which belongs to a person in whom the creditors have confidence, may be withdrawn from the operation of the law, and left in his hands. Experience has shewn that an ill-disposed or unreasonable creditor will not hesitate to force an estate into liquidation, even when circumstances prevent the possibility of the value of the assets being obtained ; and that under any circumstances whatever, it is better for the creditors to have an estate wound up by the debtor himself, if he is trustworthy. Most Bankruptcy systems have comprised a provision of this kind. See E. Act § 110. 1 Doria and Macrae, pp. 450, et seq :—S. Act § 35, et seq :—Murdoch, pp. 240, et seq :—C. Com. art. 504, et seq.

2. *To suspend further proceedings —*
This phrase is somewhat ambiguous, as is also the provision in p. 19, that such suspension when granted shall be in force for three calendar months thereafter ; as it is nowhere expressly stated what effect such suspension will have upon the pending proceedings. At the time of the presentation of the petition contemplated by this section, the writ of attachment has issued and the guardian is in possesion of the estate and effects of the debtor. Is the attachment to be put an end to and the guardian discharged ? or is the writ to remain in force and the guardian in possession for three months ? If an affirmative answer to the latter question were to be considered the correct solution of the difficulty, the proceeding which is so carefully described in pp. 15 to 21, would be worse than useless ; in fact it would be utterly ruinous to the estate ; and instead of being likely to be petitioned for, would probably meet with strenuous opposition from the debtor himself. But an examination of the provisions of the act and of the intention of these clauses, seems to point to a different conclusion.

While it is true that the word "suspend" is repeatedly used, and no express provision is made for discharging the attachment, the 19th clause prescribes the question which is to be put to the creditors. This question is "shall the debtor be proceeded against under this Act or not?" and if the decision be in the negative, it is declared that "it shall be in force" for three months thereafter; during which time no other proceedings can be taken against him, based upon anything which occurred previous to the institution of the pending proceedings. The decision in such case would therefore be that the debtor shall not be proceeded against under the Act. The obvious meaning of this provision goes beyond the more suspension of existing proceedings, if by such suspension, the continuance in force of those already taken be implied. If the debtor is not to be proceeded against, the attachment must be discharged; for to retain it in force, and the guardian in charge, would be to continue to proceed against him under the act, and to act in the very face of the resolution of the creditors.

The spirit of these clauses leads to the same conclusion. Their object evidently is to relieve the debtor from the operation of the act, which could only be done by restoring to him the possession and administration of his estate; and thus to allow him a space of three months within which to make a fresh effort to carry on his business. This intention would be entirely defeated if the attachment were not discharged.

16. The debtor shall produce with such petition a schedule of his estate, and a list of his creditors with the amount of his indebtedness to each, and the places of their respective residences, or places of business, together with particulars of any negotiable paper on which his name appears, the holders of which are unknown to him; the whole under oath ; *Schedule to be produced with the petition.*

The distinction between creditors holding direct, or overdue indirect claims and those holding indirect claims not yet matured, is not preserved by this clause, and must be presumed to be intended to be disregarded. It is of less importance, the greater the lapse of time after the stoppage of payment, as the number of immature indirect claims will diminish as the time passes.

17. Upon the schedule of the estate and the list of creditors being furnished by the debtor, sworn to as aforesaid, the judge, instead of ordering a meeting of creditors to be called for the appointment of an official assignee, shall order a meeting of creditors to be called by advertisement for the purpose of taking into consideration the prayer of such petition, and at such meeting shall take and record by a writing under his hand the opinion of the creditors thereon ; *Duty of Judge in such case.* *Meeting to be called.*

1. *By advertisement—*
As the means now exist for attaining a knowledge of the creditor's names and residences, notices must be sent to them by post according to § 11, p. 1.
2. *For the purpose of taking into consideration the prayer of the petition—*
It will be necessary to appoint an official assignee at the meeting thus ordered, if the creditors decide against the prayer of the petition, *post* p. 20. It would therefore be proper that the notice should mention as one of the purposes of the meeting, the giving of advice, if necessary, upon the appointment of an official assignee.

18. The judge shall postpone the meeting so called if it appears that the creditors have not been properly and reaso- *Postponement of meeting.*

nably notified, or that important omissions have been made in the creditors' list ;

Judge to pre-
side at such
meeting. 19. The judge shall preside at such meeting of creditors, and the question which they shall decide shall be, " Shall the debtor be proceeded against under this Act or not ?" And if the Question to be
decided there-
at, and how. decision of the majority in number and three-fourths in value of the creditors for sums above one hundred dollars, present or represented, be in the negative, it shall be in force for three calendar months thereafter, during which time no other proceedings in insolvency shall be commenced against the debtor, based upon any act or omission of his which took place previous to the institution of the proceedings so stayed by the decision of the creditors ;

1. *It shall be in force*—
See note to p. 15. – The Judge should then on application order the discharge of the attachment. The costs are payable out of the estate, § 11, p. 16 - and if the attachment be discharged would fall upon the debtor.
2. *Above one hundred dollars*—
See note to § 2, p. 2.
3. *Which took place previous*—
But the decision of the creditors would not protect the debtor from proceedings based upon any fresh act of insolvency, committed after the institution of the proceedings which had been put an end to.

Proceedings
on decision of
meeting. 20. If the decision at such meeting be not in the negative, the judge shall at once proceed thereat to take the advice of the creditors as to the appointment of an official assignee, and shall appoint such assignee as hereinbefore provided ;

In case of
question as to
amount of any
creditor's
claim. 21. If any question arises at such meeting respecting the amount of any creditor's claim, it shall be decided by the judge upon a hearing of the parties, and from an inspection of the schedules and list so sworn to by the debtor, and of the statement of the debtor's affairs prepared and produced at such meeting by the guardian, or person entrusted with the writ of attachment ;

1. *Upon a hearing of the parties and from an inspection, &c*—
It is not intended that the Judge shall hear evidence, but that he shall decide upon the evidence before him contained in the schedules and statements produced by the debtor, and the guardian.
2. *Prepared and produced by the guardian*—
As this is a meeting for the appointment of an official assignee if necessary, the provision of p. 11. that the guardian shall produce statements of the debtor's affairs at the meeting called for the appointment of an official assignee, applies to it.

Effect of ap-
pointment of
official as-
signee. 22. Upon the appointment of the official assignee, the guardian shall deliver the estate and effects attached, to the official assignee ; and by the effect of his appointment, the whole of the estate and effects of the insolvent, as existing at the date of the issue of the writ, and which may accrue to him by any title whatsoever, up to the time of his discharge under this Act, and whether seized or not seized under the writ of attachment, shall vest in the said official assignee, in the same manner and to the same extent, and with the same exceptions as if a voluntary assignment of the estate of the insolvent had been at that date executed in his favor by the insolvent ;

1. *The whole of the estate and effects —*
See the cases collected in D. & M , pp. 550, *et seq.*, and Archbold, pp. 220, *et seq.*, exhibiting the construction of similar general clauses in the English Bankruptcy Acts. See also S. act § 102, Murdoch, p. 96, Code Com. art. 443. Renouard, pp. 164 et seq. 1 Bedarride, pp. 81 et seq.

2. *As existing at t e date of the issue of the writ —*
In England the estate vests in the assignee from the time of the act of Bankruptcy. Archbold, p. 216. 1 D. & M., p. 545. In Scotland it vests in the Trustee from the date of the sequestration. S. act § 102. In France the debtor is deprived of his effects from the date of the judgment *déclaratif de la faillite.* Code Com. art. 413.

Our Statute vests the estate of the insolvent in his assignee, on the execution of a deed of assignment, or on the issue of a writ of attachment. And in this respect it is more just towards third parties than the English Act, under which injury has frequently resulted to innocent persons from having transacted business with the Bankrupt, after an act of Bankruptcy of which they were ignorant. The public notice which is required to be given in both cases here ; namely, previous to an assignment, by the Insolvent himself, § 2. p. 1 ; upon the assignment by the assignee, Form D, Rule of practice No. 22 ; and upon the issue of a writ by the Sheriff, § 3, p. 8 ; renders it impossible for any person exercising ordinary care in conducting his business, to fall into a similar difficulty in this country.

3. *Up to the time of his discharge—*
Similar provisions are to be found in the laws of England, Scotland and France ; 1 D. & M. p. 550. S. act § 103. Murdoch, p. 292 Code Com. art. 443 1 Bedarride, No. 81.

4. *Whether seized or not seized—*
It is the issue of the writ which operates the *dessaisissement* of the insolvent, and not the actual seizure by the officer. The writ is similar to the English Commission, and its issue produces the same effect in this respect as the judgment *déclaratif de la faillite,* in France.

5. *With the same exceptions —*
See note to § 2, p. 7.

6. *A voluntary assignment—*
For the effect of an assignment see § 2, p. 7.

23. An authentic copy or exemplification, under the hand of the proper officer of the Court, of the order of the Judge appointing an official assignee, may be registered at full length in any registry office, without any proof of the signature of the officer and without any memorial ; and such registration shall have the same effect as to the real estate of the insolvent and in all other respects, as the registration of a deed of assignment under this Act ;

Effect of registration of order of appointment.

As the Registration of a deed of assignment—
That is, no subsequent registration of any deed or instrument which would otherwise have affected the Insolvent's real estate will have any force or effect as regards that real estate In fact the appointment of the official assignee operates with regard to the Insolvent's real estate as a deed of sale of it would ; and its registration has the same effect as that which

a deed of sale would have, in so far as regards arresting the creation of new charges upon the real estate conveyed by it.

The absence of description of the property conveyed, can produce no injurious effect with regard to third persons, for the insolvency is public ; and as when it occurs, no one can acquire a title from the insolvent to any portion of the property held by him previous to his discharge, or even a mortgage upon it, no one can be misled by the want of a description of the property conveyed And the same result will follow even where the system prevailing with regard to registration, provides that it shall be made against the land affected by the deed enregistered, and not merely against the person obliged by that deed.

Notice of appointment.

24. Immediately upon his appointment, the official assignee shall give notice thereof by advertisement (Form K), requiring by such notice all creditors of the insolvent to produce before him their claims, and the vouchers in support thereof.

Shall give notice thereof—
A similar provision to this, requiring the assignee under a deed of assignment to give notice of his appointment and call in the creditors, appeared in the draft of the Bill submitted to the House of Assembly in 1862. The form of notice prescribed by that provision (Form D) still stands as part of the Act passed in 1864, but the clause ordering its use has disappeared. To remedy this omission the Honorable Judges in Lower Canada have very judiciously made a rule of practice directing that notice in the form D, shall be given by the assignee under a voluntary assignment, in the same manner as by the official assignee. Rule 22.

OF ASSIGNEES.

Boards of Trade may name official assignees.

S curity.

Notice of nomination.

1. The Board of Trade at any place, or the Council thereof, may name any number of persons within the County or District in which such Board of Trade exists, or within any County or District adjacent thereto in which there is no Board of Trade, to be official assignees for the purposes of this Act, and at the time of such nomination shall declare what security for the due performance of his duties, shall be given by each of such official assignees before entering upon them ; and a copy of the resolution naming such persons, certified by the Secretary of the Board, shall be transmitted to the Prothonotary or Clerk of the Court in the District or County within which such assignees are resident :

1. *The Board of Trade at any place—*
The object of this section appears to be to create a class of men, satisfactory to the Commercial community generally, and under sufficient security for the due performance of their duties, who shall always be available when a trustworthy and competent guardian or assignee is required. It is intended that one of them shall take charge of an insolvent estate as soon as it is seized, and devote himself, pending the return of the writ, to making a full examination, and intelligible and reliable statements of the debtor's affairs ; and that the Judge may have them to resort to, whenever the absence of eligible or impartial persons among those proposed by the creditors, renders it necessary for him to look elsewhere for an official assignee. If the plan indicated by this section proves successful, it will also tend to diminish the bad effect produced by appointing as assignee some large creditor, or Bank cashier, which in the one instance generally results in successful devices for the protection of the assignee's own claim ;

and in the other in burdening the estate with an assignee whose existing duties are too onerous to enable him to attend to those imposed upon him by the office, and in the consequent necessity for agents who are paid out of the estate, to enable him to earn his commission. And when it is remembered that the assignee performs the functions of arbitrator upon many disputed points, the advantage of having a professional assignee becomes manifest.

A similar mode of creating a class of men from whom assignees may be chosen prevails in England, the nomination there being made by the Lord Chancellor and the number limited to thirty. 1 D. & M., 57. Archbold, p. 205.

2. *County or District adjacent thereto—*

That is, County in Upper Canada, or District in Lower Canada, as the case may be; these being the territorial divisions marking the jurisdiction of the local Judges in each section of the Province respectively.

This clause might be held to confine the right of nomination by the several Boards of Trade, to the Counties or Districts actually adjoining that in which each is established; but such would not appear to be the intention of the Act. It would rather seem to have been contemplated that there should be official assignees nominated in every County or District, and that the Board of Trade within the most convenient distance should have the nomination. And this construction is favored by the terms of § 3, p. 10, where the word "nearest" instead of "adjacent" is used.

4. *Transmitted to the Prothonotary or Clerk—*

That an authentic list of the official assignees named may be easily accessible; and specially to the Sheriff when he requires a guardian, and to the Judge when he is called upon to appoint an assignee.

2. Such security shall be taken in the name of office of the President of such Board of Trade, for the benefit of the creditors of any person whose estate is, or subsequently may be, in process of liquidation under this Act; and in case of the default of any such assignee in the performance of his duties, his security may be enforced and realized by the assignee who shall be appointed his successor, who may sue in his own name as such assignee upon such security; *Security to be given by assignee.*

1. *Taken in the name of office—*

The bond should remain deposited in the office of the Board of Trade that any assignee desiring to proceed upon it may have access to it. For the official assignee to whom it applied might be acting for several estates, and a defaulter to each, in which case it would not be proper that any one assignee should have the possession and custody of the bond. Proof of it might be made if necessary, by the proper officer of the Board of Trade being brought up with it under a *subpœna duces tecum.*

2. *In process of liquidation—*

This would apply to estates whether under process of voluntary or compulsory liquidation.

3. The assignee shall call meetings of creditors, whenever required in writing so to do by five creditors, stating in such writing the purpose of the intended meeting; or whenever he is required so to do by the Judge, on the application of any creditor, of which application he shall have notice; or whenever he shall himself require instructions from the creditors; and he shall state succinctly in the notice calling any meeting, the purposes of such meeting; *Meeting of creditors, when to be called by assignee.*

' 1. *The assignee shall call meetings* --
Of which notice must be given in the mode indicated by § 11, p. 1.
2. *He shall have notice*—
That is one clear day, as provided by § 11, p. 9.
3. *Or whenever he shall himself require instructions*—
The act leaves in the hands of the creditors the power of regulating nearly every detail of the proceedings for the liquidation of the estate, for the protection of their own interests, and as tending to these objects, for the regulation of the conduct of the assignee. See this section, and ss. 3, 4, 6, 8, 11, 13, 16, 17, 18, 20, § 5, p. 15, § 6, p. 2, § 10, p. 1, § 11, p. 3. And it is important that the creditors should act upon the powers thus conferred upon them.
4. *And he shall state succinctly in such notice*—
The advantages that creditors might obtain by using their powers in controlling the assignee and in managing the estate, will be greatly lessened, and expense and delay will be increased, unless the assignee takes care to call any meeting that may be required, in such a manner as to enable the creditors to act at such meeting in respect of all the matters in which they have jurisdiction. For this purpose it is necessary to specify in the notice, as the purposes for which the meeting is called, the regulation of every matter which is intended to be submitted to them, and thus enable the requisite business to be done at one meeting, instead of several being necessary. The first meeting however which is held after the expiry of two months from the appointment of an assignee, may be used for the transaction of all the business the creditors can do, without such business having been detailed in the advertisement, provided a special but short form of notice is used in calling it. § 11, p. 3.

Assignee to be subject to certain rules.

Deposit of moneys.

4. The assignee shall be subject to all rules, orders and directions, not contrary to law, or to the provisions of this Act, which are made for his guidance by the creditors at a meeting called for the purpose ; and until he receives directions from the creditors in that behalf, if there be a Bank or agency of a Bank in the County in which the insolvent has his place of business, or within fifteen miles of such place, he shall deposit weekly, at interest, in the name of the estate, all moneys received by him, in the Bank or Bank-agency in or nearest to the place where the insolvent so carries on business ;

Subject to all rules, orders and directions made by the Creditors—
This is very similar to the provisions of the Scotch law ; in which like powers in the management of the estate and over the Trustee, are given to the creditors. S. act § 82, § 96. Murdoch. pp. 276, 287. The modern French law allows less weight to the vote of the creditors than does any other Bankrupt system, seldom permitting them to decide any question by a vote, and usually leaving the decision to a judicial officer, after hearing their opinions upon the matter under consideration. C. Com. art. 529 et seq. Renouard, p. 525. But the Ord. of 1673, like the Scotch law, accorded extensive powers to the creditors, (Ord. 1673, tit. 11, arts. 5, 6 and 7.) whose opinions appear to have been taken by vote at meetings held for the purpose ; and whose decisions seem to have depended upon the majority in value as well as in number,—see articles above cited and the commentary of M. Jousse. The modern English Bankrupt Act, like that of France, grants but very limited powers to the creditors.
The present act adopts the principle of the Ord. of 1673, and approaches closely in its details to the mode in which the same principle is worked out in the Scotch act. As to the Bank deposits, Rule 26 requires the assignee to file a monthly return of the moneys deposited and in his hands: and regulates the mode in which moneys deposited may be drawn.

5. The assignee shall attend all meetings of creditors, and take and preserve minutes of such meetings, signed by himself, and signed and certified at the time by the chairman, or by three creditors present at the meeting; and copies of, and extracts from, such minutes, certified by the assignee, shall be *primâ facie* evidence of the proceedings purporting to be recorded in such minutes; and he shall also keep a correct register of all his proceedings, and of all claims made to or before him; To attend all meetings of creditors.
And keep minutes, &c.

1. *The assignee shall attend all meetings—*
Similar duties to those imposed upon the assignee by this section, are performed by the Trustee under the Scotch act, § 81. Of course neither this provision nor that respecting the minutes can apply to the first meeting under proceedings for a voluntary assignment, as when it is held, no assignee is in existence. See note on § 2, p. 3.
2. *Shall be primâ facie evidence—*
Copies, certified as provided by this section, of the minutes of all meetings of creditors are required to be filed in the office of the Superior Court, Rule 25.—A record of them is required in Court whenever the Judge is called upon to enforce the directions of the creditors under § 4, p. 16.
3. *Of all his proceedings—*
As with regard to claims or dividends objected to, the preparation of dividend sheets, the dates at which all notices are given, in fact every step he takes, or that is taken before him in the case, and specially those proceedings the dates of which are of importance. And by Rule 24, the Minutes and Register of proceedings must be accessible to all persons interested during office hours.

6. The assignee shall give such security and in such manner as shall be ordered by a resolution of the creditors, and shall conform himself to such directions in respect thereof, and in respect of any change or modification thereof or addition thereto, as are subsequently conveyed to him by similar resolutions; and in every case except where the security as been taken in the name of the President of the Board of Trade, and is not required to be changed, the bond or instrument of security shall be taken in favor of the creditors, by the name of the "Creditors of A. B., an insolvent, under the Insolvent Act of 1864," and shall be deposited in the office of the Court, and in case of default by the assignee on whose behalf it is given, may be sued upon by any assignee who shall be subsequently appointed, in his own name as such assignee; Security to be given to creditors.
The Bond.
How kept.

1. *Such security as shall be ordered—*
If the creditors are satisfied with the security given by the official assignee, to the President of the Board of Trade, no resolution need be passed.
2. *And shall conform himself—*
He may be compelled at any time by a resolution of the creditors to give more or other security, or to change the terms of that already given. The penalty for disobedience however, would only be the danger of removal by the creditors. *Post* p. 18.
3. *May be sued upon—*
The remedy against the security is the same whether it be given to the President of the Board of Trade or to the creditors direct. And it is the same mode of procedure which is in use in Scotland. S. act § 72, Murdoch, p. 267. In England also the creditors regulate the nature and amount

of the security, but it is taken in favor of the Registrar of the Court, who may enforce it. E. act § 122.

Powers of insolvent vested in assignee. 7. All powers vested in any insolvent which he might legally execute for his own benefit, shall vest in, and be executed by the assignee, in like manner and with like effect as they were vested in the insolvent, and might have been executed by him; but no power vested in the insolvent or property or effects held by him as Trustee or otherwise for the benefit of others, shall vest in the assignee under this Act;

This clause may be said to be merely supplementary to § 2, p. 7, and § 3, p. 22.

Winding up affairs. 8. The assignee shall wind up the affairs of the insolvent, by the sale, in a prudent manner, of all bank and other stocks, and of all movables belonging to him, and by the collection of all debts; but in all of such respects shall be guided by the direction of the creditors, given as herein provided;

1. *Wind up the affairs of the insolvent—*
Jousse, Ord. de 1673, p. 160. C. C. art. 484 et seq. S. act § 82. Murdoch, p. 276. E. act § 127.

2. *Shall be guided by the directions of the creditors—*
This is in accordance with the old French law : Jousse, loc. cit; but under the modern system it is the *juge commissaire* who gives directions as to the winding up of the estate. C. C. loc. cit. So in Scotland it is the Commissioners. S. act § 85, Murdoch, 279. In England his duties are prescribed by § 127, and the Court will enforce their performance.
3. *Given as herein provided—*
i. e. at a meeting called for the purpose, *ante* p. 4.

Assignee's right of action, &c. 9. The assignee, in his own name as such, may sue for the recovery of all debts due to the insolvent, and may take, both in the prosecution and defence of suits, all the proceedings that the insolvent might have taken with respect to the estate, and may intervene and represent the insolvent in all suits or proceedings by or against him, which are pending at the time of his appointment, and on his application may have his name inserted therein, in the place of that of the insolvent;

When the insolvent is a partner in a trading company, &c. 10. If a partner in an unincorporated trading Company or co-partnership, becomes insolvent within the meaning of this Act, and an assignee is appointed to the estate of such insolvent, the assignee shall have all the rights of action and remedies against the other partners in such Company or co-partnership, which any partner could have or exercise by law against his co-partners after the dissolution of the firm; and may avail himself of such rights of action and remedies, as if such co-partnership or Company had expired by efflux of time;

The assignee shall have all the rights of action—
This provision embodies what is recognized in England as law on this subject. 1 D. & M. pp. 560-1. In Scotland it would seem that Bank-

ruptcy would be a valid ground of dissolution. Murdoch, pp. 53-4. 2 Bell,
643.   In France the question is one of greater difficulty, it being contended,
that though the insolvency of one copartner may be a valid reason in the
mouths of the insolvent's copartners for demanding a dissolution, it gives
neither him nor his creditors any privilege or right which he would not
have had under the agreement of copartnership. 4 Pardessus, p. 189, No.
1066. But see C. C. art 1865. 4 Duvergier, No. 443. The English and
Scotch system, though it respects in a less degree the conditions of the contract of partnership, is practically more equitable, taking the rights of all
parties into consideration; and it tends to prevent a mode of evading the
consequences of liability, and of protecting the assets of a debtor from
seizure, which was gradually assuming alarming proportions in Lower
Canada.

2. *After the dissolution of the firm*—
Bankruptcy, (*Faillite*,) of itself operates a dissolution of a partnership.
Pothier, Société, No. 148. Domat, liv. 1, t. 8, sect. 5, n. 12. Can. Code,
Partnership, No. 58. See also above cited English and Scotch authorities.
Story on Partnership, § 313. Code civ. art. 1865.

11. After having acted with due diligence in the collection *As to doubt-*
of the debts, if the assignee finds there remain debts due, the *ful debts due*
attempt to collect which would be more onerous than benefi- *estate: sale*
cial to the estate, he may report the same to the creditors at a *ed.* *may be order-*
meeting thereof duly called for the purpose ; and with their
sanction he may obtain an order of the Judge to sell the same
by public auction, after such advertisements thereof as may be
required by such order ; and pending such advertisements, the
assignee shall keep a list of the debts to be sold, open to
inspection at his office, and shall also give free access to all
documents and vouchers explanatory of such debts ; but all *Proviso:*
debts amounting to more than one hundred dollars shall be sold
separately ;

C. Com. art. 570. 2 Renouard, p. 335. Bed., Nos. 1064 et seq

12. The person who purchases a debt from the assignee, *Rights of pur-*
may sue for it in his own name as effectually as the insolvent *chaser of debt.*
might have done, and as the assignee is hereby authorized to
do ; and a bill of sale (Form L.,) signed and delivered to him
by the assignee, shall be *primâ facie* evidence of such purchase
without proof of the handwriting of the assignee ; and no war-
ranty, except as to the good faith of the assignee, shall be
created by such sale and conveyance, not even that the debt
is due ;

13. The assignee may sell the real estate of the insolvent, *Sale of insol-*
but only after advertisement thereof, for the same time and in *vent's real*
the same manner as is required for the actual advertisement of *estate: notice.*
sales of real estate by the Sheriff in the district or place where
such real estate is situate, and to such further extent as the assignee deems expedient ; but the period of advertisement may
be shortened to not less than two months by a resolution of the
creditors passed at a meeting called for the purpose, and approved of by the Judge ; and if the price offered for any real *Power to*
estate at any public sale duly advertised as aforesaid, is in the *withdraw:*
3*

and sell afterwards.

opinion of the assignee too small, he may withdraw such real estate, and sell it subsequently under such directions as he receives from the creditors ;

1. *The assignee may sell the real estate—*
There would seem to be no need of any formality of seizure or the like before advertising. And as there is no restriction as to place, it would seem that the sale may be held at any convenient place, in the discretion of the assignee.

2. *After advertisement thereof in the same manner—*
It may be doubtful whether this would require in Lower Canada the publication of the sale at the church door, as is necessary in sales by the Sheriff. Till this point is settled, therefore, it would be a prudent precaution to cause such publications to be made.

3. *And to such further extent—*
That is by advertisements in local papers, placards and similar means of giving publicity to the sale.

4. *The period of advertisement may be shortened—*
This and the requisite directions for the sale of the real estate if withdrawn, are proper matters to be disposed of at the general meeting of the creditors referred to in § 11, p. 3. See note to that clause.

5. *At any public sale—*
The first attempt at sale should be by public auction, but the subsequent sale may be by private bargain, if so ordered by the creditors.
See S. act § 114, 115. C. Com. art. 534 and art. 571 et seq.

Effect of sale of real estate by assignee in U. C. and L. C. respectively.

Credit for purchase money.

Reserving mortgage therefor.

14. The sale of real estate in Upper Canada so made by the assignee, shall have the same effect as if the same had been made by a Sheriff in Upper Canada, under a writ of execution issued in the ordinary course ; and in Lower Canada, such sales shall have the same effect as if made by a Sheriff under a similar writ ; and the deed of such sale which the assignee executes, (Form M.) shall have precisely the same effect as a Sheriff's deed has in that part of the Province within which the real estate is situate ; but he may grant such terms of credit as he may deem expedient, and as may be approved of by the creditors for any part of the purchase money ; and if no previous hypothec or mortgage remains upon such real estate, he shall be entitled to reserve a special hypothec or mortgage by the deed of sale, as security for the payment of such part of the purchase money ; and such deed may be executed before witnesses, or before Notaries, according to the exigency of the law of the place where the real estate sold is situate ;

1. *And as may be approved of by the creditors—*
This is also a matter which should be submitted to the creditors at the general meeting. See note to § 11, p. 3.

2. *And if no previous hypothec or mortgage remains—*
The previous portion of the paragraph does not limit the giving a term of credit to the cases where the assignee can obtain a first mortgage; but although this provision does not forbid the taking of any but a first mortgage, it does not seem to contemplate that any other will be taken. Practically therefore credit will seldom be given except when the property is sold free of mortgages.

Duty of assignee selling

15. In Lower Canada, before advertising any sale of real estate the assignee shall procure, at the expense of the estate, from

the Registrar of the County wherein such real estate is situate, real estate in a certificate containing the names and residences as shewn by L. C. the Registry books of all persons enregistered as hypothecary creditors upon such real estate ; and he shall himself deposit Notice to registered inin the nearest post office a notice with the postage paid thereon, cumbrancers, addressed to each of such creditors by the name and to the address contained in such certificate, and also a notice addressed to each creditor at any other place where the assignee has reason to believe such creditor to be then resident, and also a And other notice addressed to any other person whom the assignee has hypothecary reason to believe to be then the creditor of such hypothecary creditors. claim,—informing the creditors of the day fixed for the sale of the real estate, and of the time within which the hypothecary creditors are required to file their claims under this Act ; and Certificate of before the day of sale he shall file in the office of the Court the Registrar to certificate of the Registrar with a return thereon under oath as be filed. to his doings in respect of such notices ; and the assignee Liability of shall be directly liable for any neglect of the duty imposed assignee for upon him by this section, to any party suffering damage in neglect. consequence of such neglect ;

1. *Time within which the hypothecary creditors are required to file—* Within six days from the day of sale. § 11, p. 7.

16. The assignee shall be subject to the summary jurisdic- Assignee to tion of the Court or Judge in the same manner and to the be subject to same extent as the ordinary officers of the Court are subject to summary jurisdiction of its jurisdiction, and the performance of his duties may be the Court. enforced by the Judge on summary petition in vacation, or by the Court on a rule in term, under penalty of imprisonment, as for contempt of Court, whether such duties be imposed upon him by the deed of assignment, by instructions from the creditors validly passed by them under this Act and communicated to him, or by the terms of this Act ;

1. *And communicated to him—* It is the duty of the assignee to attend all meetings of creditors, and to preserve minutes of them. If he performs this duty and is present when the instructions are passed by the meeting, no further communication of them would seem to be necessary.

17. Before the period at which dividends may be declared, Removal of any assignee may be removed by the Judge, upon proof of assignee by a fraud or dishonesty in the custody or management of the estate, Judge for mis.onduct. upon the application of any creditor ; and if such removal Appointment takes place, or if the assignee dies more than fifteen days of another. before the said period, the Judge may appoint another assignee in the same manner as he can appoint an assignee to an estate in compulsory liquidation ; but if the assignee is removed or dies within fifteen days of the said period, the Judge shall order a meeting of creditors to be held for the purpose of appointing another assignee, and shall cause notice of such meeting to be given by advertisement ;

1. *Before the period—*
Viz, two months from the first publication of the appointment of the
assignee. This is the time within which the creditors are called upon to
file their claims. § 3, p. 24, Rule 22, Forms D. and K.
Until this period expires, there is not supposed to be any satisfactory
mode of ascertaining the amount of the claims of creditors which may
be voted on, and the power of removal is therefore left with the Judge.
2. *Within fifteen days—*
Because that is the shortest period of time within which a meeting could be
called.—The creditors will then have proved their claims, and means will
exist for ascertaining the precise proportions in number and value of those
that vote.

Removal of
assignee by
creditors.

Appointment
of another.

18. Any assignee may be removed after the period at which
dividends may be declared, by a resolution passed by the
creditors present or represented at a meeting duly called for
the purpose ; and if the removal has been effected by an order
of the Judge, or if the assignee dies within fifteen days before
the said period, or if the removal is effected by the creditors
after the said period, they shall have the right of appointing
another assignee, either at the meeting by which he is removed,
or at any other called for the purpose ;

1. *Any assignee may be removed—*
It does not appear necessary that any reason for the removal should be
stated, or proved to exist.
2. *Resolution passed—*
That is upon the principle of computing the votes provided for by § 11, p. 2.
3. *Within fifteen days—*
These words must apply to the case of removal by order of the Judge, as
well as to the case of the assignee dying ; as if such order of removal is
made more than fifteen days before the period mentioned, the Judge himself appoints another assignee. *Ante* p. 17.

Assignee re-
moved to re-
main account-
able.

19. The assignee so removed shall, nevertheless, remain
subject to the summary jurisdiction of the Court, and of any
Judge thereof, until he shall have fully accounted for his acts
and conduct while he continued to be assignee ;

Remuneration
of assignee.

20. The remuneration of the assignee shall be fixed by the
creditors at a meeting called for the purpose ; but if not so fixed
before a final dividend is declared, shall be put into the dividend sheet at a rate not exceeding five *per centum* upon the
cash receipts, subject to objection by any creditor as exceeding
the value of the services of the assignee, in the same manner as
any other item of the dividend sheet ;

What shall be
done with the
estate in the
event of his
death.

21. Upon the death of an assignee the estate of the insolvent
shall not descend to the heirs or representatives of the assignee,
but shall become vested in any assignee who shall be appointed
by the creditors in his place and stead ; and until the new
assignee is appointed, the estate shall be under the control of
the Judge ;

How assignee
may obtain
his discharge.

22. After the declaration of a final dividend the assignee
may prepare his final account, and after due notice by adver-

tisement may present a petition to the Judge for his discharge
from the office of assignee ; and from the time of the first
advertisement thereof, to the time of the presentation of such
petition, he shall keep such final account open for inspection
at his office ;

23. The assignee shall produce and file with such petition
a bank certificate of the deposit of any dividends remaining
unclaimed, or of any balance in his hands, and thereupon the
Judge, after hearing the parties, may refuse, or grant conditionally or unconditionally, the prayer of such petition.

Assignee to file a certificate with his petition for discharge.

1. *Dividends remaining unclaimed—*
See § 5, p. 17.
2. *The parties—*
Any of the creditors, the insolvent, and the assignee.
3. *Conditionally or unconditionally—*
One condition undoubtedly should be, that he should make up the record
of proceedings by and before him as assignee, and deposit it in the Court,
together with the minutes of the meetings of creditors and his register of
proceedings, with a correct list of the whole.

OF DIVIDENDS.

5. Upon the expiration of the period of two months from the
first insertion of the advertisements giving notice of an assignment, or of the appointment of an official assignee, or as soon
as may be after the expiration of such period, and afterwards
from time to time at intervals of not more than six months,
the assignee shall prepare and keep constantly accessible to
the creditors, accounts and statements of his doings as such
assignee, and of the position of the estate and at similar
intervals shall prepare dividends of the estate of the insolvent :

Accounts to be kept and dividends pre- pared by as- signee.

1. *Two months—*
As soon as the assignee is appointed he must give notice of the fact by
advertisement, and call upon all creditors to file their claims within two
months from the first insertion of such advertisement. § 3, p. 24, Forms D.
and K. Rule 22. And during the same interval it will be the duty of the
assignee to proceed with the realization of the assets of the estate, and with
the investigation of its real condition. As it may reasonably be expected
that during this period the greater portion of the creditors will have filed
their claims, at its termination the assignee should be able to attain a very
close approximation to the actual position of its affairs. And he is therefore then required to lay before the creditors the information he has obtained.
For these reasons also, this is the time fixed for the first general meeting of
creditors, when all the regulations required for the guidance of the assignee
may be passed. § 11, p. 3. In Scotland four months are allowed for
similar purposes. S. Act, § 125. Kinnear, pp. 145 *et seq.*
2. *Similar intervals—*
That is of not more than six months, but he should declare dividends as
often as he has funds to divide.

2. All debts due and payable by the insolvent at the time of
the execution of a deed of assignment, or at the time of the
issue of a writ of attachment under this Act, and all debts due

What debts may rank for payment out

but not then actually payable, subject to such rebate of interest as may be reasonable, shall have the right to rank upon the estate of the insolvent ; and any person then being as surety or otherwise liable for any debt of the insolvent who subsequently pays such debt, shall stand in the place of the original creditor, if such creditor has proved his claim on such debt ; or if he has not proved shall be intitled to prove against and rank upon the estate for such debt, to the same extent and with the same effect as such creditor might have done ;

1. *At the time of the execution of a deed of assignment*—
Debts incurred afterwards would not be proveable, and therefore the insolvent would not be relieved from them by a discharge under the act. Although all assets acquired up to the time of the discharge are vested in the assignee. § 3, p. 22, § 2, p. 9. Renouard, No. 89. Pardessus, No. 1117. 3 Locré, p. 70. 1 Boulay-Paty, No. 67.
2. *Rebate*—
This is the ordinary rule. 2 D. & M., p. 809. Murdoch, p. 253.
3. *Reasonable*—
The only reasonable mode of arriving at the rebate, is to adopt the date of the deed of assignment, or of the appointment of the official assignee, as the period from which it is to be calculated.
4. *As such creditor might have done*—
That is after the surety has paid the debt, but not before.
These rules with regard to sureties are similar to those in force in England, France and Scotland. 2 D. & M., p. 838. Murdoch, p. 255. 12 and 13 Vict. cap. 173. Archbold, 154. C. Com. art. 544. 2 Bedarride, Nos. 881, 882. And they are strictly in accordance with the principles of our Common law.

3. If any creditor of the insolvent claims upon a contract dependent upon a condition or contingency, which does not happen previous to the declaration of the first dividend, a dividend shall be reserved upon the amount of such conditional or contingent claim until the condition or contingency is determined ; but if it be made to appear to the judge that such reserve will probably retain the estate open for an undue length of time, he may, unless an estimate of the value thereof be agreed to between the claimant and the assignee, order the assignee to make an award upon the value of such contingent or conditional claim, and thereupon the assignee shall make an award after the same investigation, and in the same manner and subject to a similar appeal, as is hereinafter provided for the making of awards upon disputed claims and dividends, and for appeals from such awards ; and in every such case the value so established or agreed to shall be ranked upon as a debt payable absolutely ;

1. *Dependent upon a condition or contingency*—
The contingency or condition may affect the amount of the debt, as in the case of a *rente viagère* or annuity ; or the existence of the debt, as in the case of a debt payable only in the event of the creditor surviving the debtor ; or merely the time of payment, as in the case of a debt payable upon the death of another. In such cases the rule to be applied in estimating the value of the claim would be different, but may be discovered, and a sufficiently accurate result obtained. This provision will most frequently

be called into operation by claims made by wives upon their husband's estates for sums of money settled upon them in lieu of dower, and payable only in case of their surviving their husbands. Unless the judgment in the case of the Bank of Montreal vs. Leslie, and Delisle, opposant, be maintained, deciding that such claims cannot rank at all upon the debtors estate, the value of such claims will have to be ascertained by a comparison of the value of the lives of the husband and wife, according to Life Assurance tables or other reliable *data*.

2. *Award after the same investigation—*
See post p. 13.

3. *Ranked upon—*
And voted upon, and computed as the value of the claimants demand, in all calculations of the proportionate value of creditor's claims. If a dividend has been previously reserved upon the full amount of the claim, it should revert to the estate, giving the creditor his dividends from the first, upon the estimated value. These provisions with regard to estimating the value of contingent or conditional claims, are similar to those acted upon in England and Scotland. Murdoch, pp. 253 et seq. 2 D. & M , 847.

4. In the preparation of the dividend sheet due regard shall be had to the rank and privilege of every creditor, which rank and privilege, upon whatever they may legally be founded, shall not be disturbed by the provisions of this Act; but no dividend shall be paid to any creditor holding collateral security from the Insolvent for his claim, until the amount for which he shall rank as a creditor on the estate as to dividends therefrom, shall be established as hereinafter provided ; and such amount shall be the amount which he shall be held to represent in voting at meetings of creditors, and in computing the proportion of creditors, whenever under this Act such proportion is required to be ascertained ;

Preparation of dividend sheet.

Creditors holding collateral security.

1. *Shall be paid—*
But the dividend should be reserved pending the adjustment of the amount for which the creditor is to rank.

2. *Hereinafter—*
See next clause.

3. *In voting at meetings--*
This really places the creditor's vote upon a proper footing. For if a creditor could vote upon the nominal amount of his claim without reference to his security, the hypothecary creditors would often control the management of the personal property, without being interested in it to any considerable extent. See note to next clause.

5. A creditor holding security from the Insolvent, or from his estate, shall specify the nature and amount of such security in his claim, and shall therein on his oath put a specified value on such security ; and the assignee, under the authority of the creditors, may either consent to the retention of such security by the creditor at such specified value, or he may require from such creditor an assignment and delivery of such security, at an advance of ten per centum upon such specified value, to be paid by him out of the estate so soon as he has realized such security, in which he shall be bound to the exercice of ordinary diligence ; and in either of such cases the difference between the value at which the security is retained or assumed and the

Duty of such secured creditors, and power of assignee.

amount of the claim of such creditor, shall be the amount for which he shall rank and vote as aforesaid ;

1. *Holding security from the Insolvent—*
A creditor who holds security derived from other sources than the insolvent or his estate, is not bound to specify it in his claim, or put a value on it It is only when it proceeds from the insolvent that his creditors are interested in it. Ex parte Parr, 1 Rose, 76. D. & M., p. 864. S. act § 59, 60.

2. *May either consent to the retention of such security—*
In France the assignee can only demand an assignment of the security, upon paying the debt. In England he has no such right under any circumstances. The rule in our act is taken from that which prevails in Scotland, and which appears more advantageous to the estate than that of France or England, and perfectly just towards the creditor. If he be left to realise the security, the sale of it would too often be a mere device to convert it to his own use at a nominal price. If it be taken from him and realised for his benefit by the assignee, the expense of the sale, and the depreciation of value which follows from seizure, would greatly diminish the proceeds. But if the creditor be required to put a value upon it on oath, with the privilege to the assignee of taking it from him at a small advance upon such valuation, as an additional check upon its correctness ; there will be a probability that the right of property in the security will finally pass from the estate at its fair value, and without much expense. Under all these systems the creditor is only permitted to rank for the balance due him after the deduction of the proceeds of his security. C. Com. act 546 *et seq.*, and 552 *et seq.* 3 Bedarride, pp. 2 *et seq.*, and 48 *et seq.* 2 Renouard, pp. 387 *et seq.* E. act 1849, § 184. D. & M., pp. 863 *et seq.* Archbold, pp. 160 *et seq.* Murdoch, pp. 256 *et seq*, 260 *et seq.*

3. *Under the authority of the creditors—*
This can only be given at a meeting, and should be one of the subjects discussed at the first general meeting.

4. *Paid out of the estate so soon as he has realized—*
The assignee is not bound to pay for the security in cash, but only when he has realized it ; in doing which he is bound to use ordinary diligence, and if he does not, may be forced on by the Judge. But on the other hand he must pay the price fixed out of the estate, whether the amount be realized from the security or not.

How creditors shall rank for payment of claims. 6. The amount due to a creditor upon each separate item of his claim at the time of the assignment, or of the appointment of the official assignee, as the case may be, shall form part of the amount for which he shall rank upon the estate of the insolvent, until such item of claim be paid in full, except in cases of deduction of the proceeds of collateral security as hereinbefore provided ; but no claim or part of a claim shall be permitted to be ranked upon more then once, whether the claim so to rank be made by the same person or by different persons ;

1. *The amount due * * at the time of the assignment—*
The time at which the assignee is appointed, whether by a deed, or by the Judge, is the common starting point of all the claims. And the amount then due upon each item of the claim, may be ranked upon, (except where deductions are made in respect of security,) until the estate is wound up, or till such item of claim is paid in full. For instance, if a creditor holds several notes or bills bearing the insolvent's name as endorser, and other and different names of persons liable before him, such creditor may rank for the amount due upon all the paper, at the date of the appointment of the assignee, and may continue to do so until the estate is fully liquidated ; unless in the interim one of the bills should be paid by one of the parties

liable before the insolvent, in which case the ranking on that item of claim would cease. See a similar rule laid down in Ex parte Groom, 3 M & A., 157. It is with reference to this provision that power is given to the assignee to demand a supplementary oath. § 11, p. 6.

2. *Ranked upon more than once—*
The questions arising upon double ranking, are sometimes intricate, but the principle is simple. When once a claim has drawn a dividend from the estate, it cannot be permitted to rank for the same dividend a second time. And this rule cannot be evaded by any device whatever, though the debt may be apparently different; as when proof is made on the consideration of a bill, after the bill has ranked; or when the creditor is changed, as by making proof by an endorser after the holder has proved.

7. If the insolvent owes debts both individually and as a member of a co-partnership, or as a member of two different co-partnerships, the claims against him shall rank first upon the estate by which the debts they represent were contracted, and shall only rank upon the other after all the creditors of that other have been paid in full ; *In case insolvent owes individually and as co-partner.*

1. *Individually and as a member of a copartnership—*
The creditors of an individual debtor could never rank upon the property of a firm of which he was a member concurrently with the creditors of such firm, for a debt due by him individually and separately, but on the other hand, until lately, the creditors of a copartnership could rank upon the estate of one of the partners, concurrently with the creditors of such partner. See Montgomery vs. Gerrard, Stuart's reports, p. 437, and the authorities collected there ; and Ex parte Gordon, 2 Rev. de jur., p. 407. 2 Boulay-Paty, No. 372 *et seq.* This rule was changed by the 22nd Vict. cap. 4, § 1. Con. Stat. L. C. p. 535, which statute is followed in the foregoing clause.

8. The creditors, or the same proportion of them that may grant a discharge to the debtor under this Act, may allot to the insolvent by way of allowance, any sum of money, or any property they may think proper ; and the allowance so made shall be inserted in the dividend sheet, and shall be subject to contestation like any other item of collocation therein, but only on the ground of fraud or deceit in procuring it, or of the absence of consent by a sufficient proportion of the creditors ; *Allowance to insolvent*

1. *The same proportion of them —*
§ 9, p. 1.

9. No costs incurred in suits against the Insolvent after due notice of an assignment or of the issue of a writ of attachment in compulsory liquidation has been given according to the provisions of this Act, shall rank upon the estate of the insolvent ; but all the taxable costs incurred in proceedings against him up to that time, shall be added to the demand for the recovery of which such proceedings were instituted ; and shall rank upon the estate as if they formed part of the original debt ; *No costs in suits against insolvent allowed after notice.*

Due notice—
That is, "by advertisement" according to § 11, p. 1.

10. Clerks, and other persons in the employ of the Insolvent in and about his business or trade, shall be collocated in the *How clerks and servants*

shall rank for wages.

dividend sheet by special privilege for any arrears of salary or wages due and unpaid to them at the time of the execution of a deed of assignment or of the issue of a writ of attachment under this Act, not exceeding three months of such arrears ;

1. *By special privilege—*
That is, out of the proceeds of the moveable property affected by such privilege as the law stands. And if there be a conflict of privilege, it will be decided by the law applicable thereto. *Ante p.* 4. And it would seem that under the law the Clerks and persons engaged about the business of the Insolvent are only privileged upon the goods in which he traded. C. C. C. Can. Priv. et Hyp. art. 32.

2. *Arrears due and unpaid at the time—*
The engagements of all persons in the employ of the insolvent cease upon the execution of an as-ignment, or the issue of a writ of attachment. And their privilege is restricted to wages actually due, no allowance for the sudden cessation of their employment being permitted. This seems to be in accordance with the former law. Earl vs. Casey, 4 L. C. Rep., 174. Poutré vs. Poutré, 6 L. C. Rep , 463. And it is the same in France. C. Com art. 549. And in Scotland. S. act § 122. And in England, D. & M., 796.

3. *Not exceeding three months—*
This restricts very much the period for which a privilege is allowed by the Common law, which is understood to be two years. See C. C. of Can., *loc. cit.* In Scotland it extends only to one month's arrears, in England to three months, and in France to six. (See authorities cited in last note.)

Notice of dividend sheet.

11. So soon as a dividend sheet is prepared, notice thereof (Form X) shall be given by advertisement, and after the expiry of six juridical days from the day of the last publication of such advertisement, all dividends which have not been objected to within that period shall be paid ;

See for similar provisions S. Act § 127 ; Murdoch, p. 305.

Provision in case it appears that all the creditors have not filed claims.

12. If it appears to the assignee on his examination of the books of the insolvent or otherwise, that the insolvent has ordinary, hypothecary or privileged creditors who have not filed claims before such assignee, it shall be his duty to reserve dividends for such creditors according to the nature of the claims, and to notify them of such reserve, which notification may be by letter through the post, addressed to such creditor's residence as nearly as the same can be ascertained by the assignee ; and if such creditors do not file their claims and apply for such dividends previous to the declaration of the last dividend of the estate, the dividends reserved for them shall form part of such last dividend ;

1. *Hypothecary—*
This must mean hypothecary creditors who have not registered. As those who have registered their *hypothèques*, will have received notice under § 4, p. 15.

2. *And apply for such dividends—*
This should not be construed to mean that if the creditor does not demand his dividend as well as file his claim, he will be deprived of it ; for that would place this class of creditors in a different position from all others. But the filing of the claim should be held to be an application for a dividend

under this clause.   And if the creditor does not afterwards claim the amount awarded him, it will follow the rule as to unclaimed dividends, established *post* p. 17.

13. If any dividend be objected to, within the said period of Case of objec-six days, and any dispute arises between the creditors of the tions to or insolvent or between him and any creditor, as to the correct disputes con- amount of the claim of any creditor, or as to the ranking or dends pro-privilege of the claim of any creditor upon such dividend sheet, vided for. the assignee shall obtain from the creditor whose claim or ranking is disputed, his statements and vouchers in duty to ex-support thereof, and from the Insolvent or opposing creditor, amine, &c. a statement showing his pretensions as to the amount thereof, and shall hear and examine the parties and their witnesses under oath, which oath the assignee is hereby empowered to administer; and shall take clear notes in writing of the parole evidence adduced before him, and shall examine and verify the statements submitted to him, by the books and accounts of the Insolvent and by such evidence, vouchers and statements as may be furnished to him ; and shall make an award in the premises, and as to the costs of such contestation, which award shall be deposited in the Court and shall be final, unless appealed from within three days from the date of its communication to the parties to the dispute ;

1. *The assignee shall obtain* * * * *statements and vouchers—*
Whether the word "statements" is to be construed as meaning "allegations" or not, it would be for the advantage of all parties, if the conflicting pretensions of the parties were required to be in writing : and accordingly it is so ordered by Rule 8. Not only is the assignee to award upon these pretensions, but they may require to be discussed before a Judge, and even in the higher Courts of Appeal ; and written statements will be absolutely necessary there to enable the question at issue to be satisfactorily disposed of. In fact if the matter in dispute be of any importance, Counsel should be employed to settle the issues, if not to conduct the case before the assignee.

2. *Shall hear and examine the parties, and their witnesses under oath—*
That is shall do so in the manner usual in litigation, observing the ordinary and reasonable rules as to evidence, of which the following may be stated as of the highest practical importance, and as requiring to be referred to, oftenest in ordinary cases :

1. That the burden of proof shall be upon him who affirms a proposition of fact, rather than upon him who denies it ;

2. That the party upon whom is the burthen of proof, shall begin ;

3. That the party who begins shall have the right to adduce evidence in rebuttal ; but that such evidence shall only be such as tends to destroy the case of his opponent, and not such as tends directly to sustain his own ;

4. That the party who holds the negative cannot usually adduce evidence in reply to his adversary's evidence in rebuttal ;

5. That if the parties are examined they cannot make evidence for themselves ; but that their answers cannot be divided ;

6. That the best evidence of which the case is susceptible should be adduced, and that secondary evidence should not be received until proof is made that the best evidence cannot be obtained ;

7. That on the examination of a witness in chief, leading questions are

not usually permissible ; but may be put on cross examination. This rule however may be reversed if the witness is plainly hostile to the party who produces him, and favorable to his opponent.

It would be obviously impossible here, to enter into a detailed discussion of the law of evidence, but enough has been said to indicate the order in which the proceedings should be carried on before the assignee. If the dispute be conducted by Counsel, the assignee will be called upon to decide questions as to the admissibility of evidence, and as to the propriety of questions put to witnesses, which might raise doubts even in the mind of a Judge accustomed to deal with them. In such cases, if the objection be to the admissibility of evidence, it would be better for the assignee to admit it, entering the objection to its admission. If it be to the propriety of a question, it is better to permit it to be put, if the assignee has any doubt, entering the objection ; and if it be an objection to the form of the question, it is always safe to insist that the question shall be so framed as to leave the facts to be related by the witness, and not put into his mouth by the questioner. And the assignee should always recollect that it is easy afterwards to disregard testimony improperly admitted ; but that the exclusion of that which ought to have been let in, is not susceptible of so simple a remedy.

3. *Clear notes in writing*—

This is an important part of the duties of the assignee ; and he is required by Rule 8 to cause such notes when taken to be signed by the witness, when he swears to them—and they should also be certified by himself as having been sworn before him.

4. *Make an award*—

The award should recite in general terms the observance of all the formalities prescribed by this clause, according to the laws respecting awards.

5. *Within three days*—

See note to § 7, p. 4.

6. *Of its communication*—

The assignee should communicate it to both parties immediately upon its being rendered and deposited. The making it in triplicate ; sending a part to each litigant, and depositing the third in Court, would be a satisfactory mode of performing this duty.

Execution of his award.   14. The award of the assignee as to costs, may be made executory by execution in the same manner as an ordinary judgment of the Court, by an order of the Judge upon the application of the party to whom costs are awarded made after notice to the opposite party ;

Costs of contesting any claim, &c.   15. The creditors may by resolution authorize and direct the costs of the contestation of any claim or any dividend to be paid out of the estate, and may make such order either before or pending any such contestation ;

Before or pending—

This does not seem to forbid such an order being made after the contestation, as the first part of the clause is general. But it appears to be intended only to remove doubts as to the power of the creditors to make an order having a prospective effect, when the amount for which the estate is bound by such order, is uncertain.

Pending appeal.   16. Pending any appeal, the assignee shall reserve a dividend equal to the amount of dividend claimed ;

Unclaimed dividends,-   17. All dividends remaining unclaimed at the time of the discharge of the assignee shall be left in the bank where they are deposited for three years, and if still unclaimed, shall then **how dealt** be paid over by such bank with the interest accrued thereon, to **with.** the Provincial Government, and if afterwards duly claimed shall be paid over to the persons entitled thereto, with interest at the rate of three per centum per annum from the time of the reception thereof by the Government ;

18. If any balance remains of the estate of the insolvent, or **Balance of es-** of the proceeds thereof, after the payment in full of all debts **tate after pay-** due by the Insolvent, such balance shall be paid over to the **ment of debts.** Insolvent upon his petition to that effect, duly notified to the creditors by advertisement and granted by the Judge.

OF LEASES.

6. If the insolvent holds under a lease property having a **How unex-** value above and beyond the amount of any rent payable under **pired leases** such lease, the assignee shall make a report thereon to the **held by the insolvent,** Judge, containing his estimate of the value of the estate of the **shall be dealt** leased property in excess of the rent ; and thereupon the Judge **with if the** may order the rights of the insolvent in such leased premises **rent be less** to be sold, after notice by advertisement of such sale ; and at **of the pre-** the time and place appointed such lease shall be sold, upon **mises.** such conditions, as to the giving of security to the lessor, as the **Sale of his** Judge may order ; and such sale shall be so made subject to **interest.** the payment of the rent and to all the covenants and conditions contained in the lease ; and all such covenants and conditions shall be binding upon the lessor and upon the purchaser, as if the purchaser had been himself lessee and a party with the lessor to the lease :

1. *If the insolvent holds under a lease—*
This is a most important chapter, innovating to a very extensive degree upon the rights of the lessor. But such a change in the law was necessary, for a lessor might absorb a very large portion or all of the assets in his premises, by insisting upon payment of his rent to the termination of the lease, perhaps some years in advance ; while the property thus paid for would be a burthen rather than an advantage to the estate.
2. *Having a value above and beyond the rent—*
Often resulting from improvements made by the insolvent with his own funds, especially under long leases.
3. *The Judge may order—*
That is if he is of opinion that the excess of value over rent, is sufficient to render it probable that a profit will be realized by such sale.
4. *The giving of security to the lessor—*
The lessor should not be compelled to accept a tenant affording him less security for his rent than he previously possessed. Therefore, if the purchaser of the lease be unable to furnish the premises with moveables sufficient to secure the rent, as effectually as it had been secured by the insolvent, or at least to a reasonable extent, the Judge should order further security to be given for it.

2. If the insolvent holds under a lease extending beyond the **Unexpired** year current under its terms at the time of his insolvency, **leases not** property which is not subject to the provisions of the last pre- **within the**

preceding section.

ceding section, or respecting which the Judge does not make an order of sale, as therein provided, the creditors shall decide at any meeting which may be held more than three months before the termination of the yearly term of the lease current at the time of such meeting, whether the property so leased should be retained for the use of the estate, only up to the end of the then current, or if the conditions of the lease permit of further extension, also up to the end of the next following yearly term thereof, and their decision shall be final ;

1. *Current under its terms*—
That is the current year of the lease, not the current year of the calendar.
2. *Property which is not subject*—
That is, property which is not of greater annual value than the rent stipulated to be paid for it ; or not of an annual value so much greater as to induce the Judge to make an order for the sale of the lease.
3. *More than three months*—
So that if they decide to give it up, the landlord may have the last three months of the current yearly term, within which to obtain a new tenant for the following year.
4. *Up to the end of the next following yearly term.*
They are not permitted to retain the property for any broken period of a new year, but must hold it for the whole year, or not at all.

Cancelling the lease, and right of the lessor in such case.

3. From and after the time fixed for the retention of the leased property for the use of the estate, the lease shall be cancelled and shall from thenceforth be inoperative and null ; and so soon as the resolution of the creditors as to such retention has been passed, such resolution shall be notified to the lessor, and if he contends that he will sustain any damage by the termination of the lease under such decision, he may make a claim for such damage, specifying the amount thereof under oath, in the same manner as in ordinary claims upon the estate ; and the assignee shall proceed forthwith to make an award upon such claim, in the same manner, and after similar investigation and with the same right of appeal as is herein provided for in the case of claims or dividends objected to ;

1. *Fixed*—
By the creditors, under the last preceding clause.
2. *To make an award*—
It is not necessary apparently that the claim should be contested before the assignee commences the proceedings for his award ; but it may be contested like any other claim, and probably should be, if considered excessive, in order that there may be a party to conduct the case against the lessor.

Measure of damages to lessor.

4. In making such claim, and in any award thereupon, the measure of damages shall be the difference between the value of the premises leased when the lease terminates under the resolution of the creditors, and the rent which the Insolvent had agreed by the lease to pay during its continuance ; and the chance of leasing or of not leasing the premises again, for a like rent, shall not enter into the computation of such damages ; and if damages are finally awarded to the lessor he shall rank for the amount upon the estate as an ordinary creditor.

1. *Measure of damages —*

All the other continuing contracts of the insolvent are terminated by his insolvency, without opening claims for damages for their non-performance ; and it seems difficult to find a good reason why the contract of lease of property, should form an exception. By this clause, therefore, the claim for damage is restricted to the actual diminution in the value of the premises, below the rent stipulated. The claim for damage even in this limited form, would scarcely be sustainable in principle, were it not that the creditors have the right under p. 1, of benefiting by any increased value, and therefore may·perhaps be held in fairness bound to submit to a claim for any diminution.

2. *He shall rank for the amount —*

The rent of the premises during the current yearly term, must be paid in full, if the goods in the premises suffice for that purpose, or if the premises are occupied by the assignee for the estate. And if they are retained for any subsequent term, the rent must be paid in full ; but the damage awarded is only a common debt, without privilege.

OF APPEAL

7. There shall be an appeal to the Judge from the award of an assignee made under this Act, which appeal shall be by summary petition of which notice shall be given to the opposite party and to the assignee ; and the assignee' shall attend before the Judge at the time and place indicated in such notice, and shall produce before him all evidence, notes of evidence, books, or proved extracts from books, documents, vouchers or papers having reference to the matter in dispute ; and thereupon the Judge may confirm such award, or modify it, or refer it back to the assignee for the taking of further evidence, by such order as will satisfy the ends of justice :

Proceedings in appeal from award of assignee.

1. *Summary Petition —*

Which should set forth the matter in issue, as already set forth in the statements of the parties before the assignee.

2. *Notice should be given —*

One clear juridical day's notice ; and only three days are allowed for appealing from the award of an assignee, (§ 5, p. 13.) A question arises upon the terms of this limitation of the time for appeal, whether the service upon the opposite party of a petition and notice in appeal, within three days from the date of the communication of the award, will satisfy the condition that it shall be " appealed from " within three days ; or whether the petition must actually be presented within the three days, to satisfy that condition. The former construction would seem to be most reasonable, and not to be inconsistent with the ordinary practice of the Courts. For if an action may properly be said to be instituted so soon as a writ has issued, requiring the defendant to appear on a future day to answer the demand of the plaintiff ; so also a judgment may be said to be appealed from, so soon as the appellant has taken the proceeding prescribed by law, for causing the respondent to appear at a future day before the tribunal in appeal, to sustain the judgment.

3. *Thereupon —*

That is of course, after hearing the parties.

2. If any of the parties to such appeal are dissatisfied with such order of the Judge, they may appeal from his judgment in Lower Canada to the Court of Queen's Bench for Lower Canada on the Appeal Side thereof, and in Upper Canada to

And on appeal from decision of the Judge.

4

Appeal must be allowed.

As to appeal to a single Judge in U. C.

either of the Superior Common Law Courts or to the Court of Chancery, or to any one of the Judges of the said Courts ; first obtaining the allowance of such appeal in Lower Canada by a Judge of the Superior Court, and in Upper Canada by a Judge of any of the Courts to which such appeal may be made ; and in either case the Judge shall be guided in allowing the same by the amount to which the assets of the estate may be affected by the final decision of the question at issue, as well as by his opinion upon the pretensions of the appellant ; but any appeal to a single Judge in Upper Canada may in his discretion be referred, on a special case to be settled, to the full Court, and on such terms in the meantime as he may think necessary and just ;

1. *They may appeal—*
There is now, however, in Lower Canada, an intermediate Court of revision created by the 27 and 28 Vict., cap. 39, and this Court has jurisdiction in matters of insolvency under p. 7, *post.*

2. *To any one of the Judges of the said Courts—*
In Upper Canada, a Judge of an inferior tribunal being entrusted with original jurisdiction in Insolvency, and with appellate jurisdiction when the assignee has decided in the first instance, an appeal is given from him to one Judge of the highest Courts of original jurisdiction. But such Judge has the power of referring the points in dispute to the full Court. See this clause *post.* In Lower Canada it is the Judges of the highest Court of original jurisdiction who are entrusted with the management of matters in Insolvency.

3. *Guided in allowing the same—*
The amount claimed could not be made a test of jurisdiction in appeal, for the interest of the estate and of the claimant, may be less upon a large claim, if the dividend is small, than upon a claim of small amount where the estate has large assets. The amount of actual interest therefore is made of weight in deciding the question of the allowance of an appeal, and upon this and his opinion of the merits of the appeal itself, the Judge is required to decide upon the application for its allowance.
It is not of course intended that the Judge should refuse the appeal merely because his opinion is adverse to the pretensions of the appellant, unless the case be one in which the appellant is plainly wrong, and where the appeal can have no other effect than to keep open the estate. If the question appealed upon, be sustainable by a reasonable argument, or the correctness of the judgment be susceptible of a reasonable doubt, and if the amount imperilled be sufficiently large to justify it, the appeal should be allowed.

Notice of appeal must be given within a certain period.

And security.

3. Such appeal shall not be permitted unless the party desiring to appeal applies for the allowance of the appeal, with notice to the opposite party, within five days from the day on which the judgment of the Judge is rendered, nor unless within five days after the allowance thereof, he causes to be served upon the opposite party and upon the assignee, a petition in appeal setting forth the petition to the Judge, and his decision thereon, and praying for its revision, with a notice of the day on which such petition is to be presented, and also within the said period of five days causes security to be given before the Judge by two sufficient sureties, that he will duly prosecute such appeal, and pay all costs incurred by reason thereof by the respondent ;

4. The petition in appeal, when the appeal is to a Court, Presenting of shall be presented on one of the first four days of the term next petition in appeal. following the putting in of the security in appeal, and shall not be thereafter received ; and when the appeal is to a Judge, the petition shall be presented within ten days after putting in security, and shall not thereafter be received ; and on or before Filing documents. the day of the presentation of the petition, the assignee shall file in the office of the Court of Appeal, or of the Court to which the Judge appealed to belongs, the evidence, papers, and documents which had been previously produced before the Judge, and thereupon the appeal shall be proceeded with and decided according to the practice of the Court ;

1. *The Petition in Appeal*—
That is to say, in appeal from the decision of a Judge, rendered upon petition to revise the award of an assignee.
2. *When the appeal is to a Judge*—
That is, to a Judge of one of the higher Courts in Upper Canada, from the decision of a Judge of the County Court.

5. If the party appellant does not present his petition on the In case petition is not day fixed for that purpose, the Court or Judge selected to be presented in appealed to as the case may be, shall order the record to be due time. returned to the assignee, and the party respondent may on the following or any other day during the same term produce before the Court, or within six days thereafter before such Judge, the copy of petition served upon him, and obtain costs thereon against the appellant ;

6. The costs in appeal shall be in the discretion of the Court Costs in appeal. or of the Judge appealed to, as the case may be ;

In the discretion of the Court—
As there is provision for a tariff of costs, (§ 11, pp. 17, 18,) this discretion is probably only intended to be exercised upon the question, whether a party shall pay costs or not, and not upon the *quantum* of such costs.

7. In Lower Canada any order of a Judge made under any Decision of of the foregoing sub-sections, shall be subject to review under one Judge in the provisions of any Act passed during the present Session, in L. C. to be subject to the same manner and upon the same conditions as judgments review. of the Superior Court for Lower Canada ; and in such cases the provisions respecting appeal to the Court of Queen's Bench hereinbefore made, shall apply to the judgments of the Court of Review.

Subject to review—
The Act 27 and 28 Vict., cap. 39, creates a Court of review, to which this clause will apply.

OF FRAUD AND FRAUDULENT PREFERENCES.

The legislation of France on the subject of the fraudulent disposition of the estate of an insolvent debtor, has varied very considerably since the well known Edict of 1609. That law declared absolutely null all *transports,*
4*

cessions, ventes et aliénations made to the children, presumptive heirs, and
friends of the debtor ; and also provided that, if these transactions were
entered into—*" faites et acceptées"*—in fraud of the creditors—the persons
engaged in them should be punished as accomplices of the bankrupt.
This provision would seem to disregard the question whether the acquisition was gratuitous or *à titre onéreux ;* and, in so far as regarded the effect of
the transaction, whether or no there was the *consilium fraudis* on the part
of either of the contracting parties. In practice however, there is no doubt
that the rule of the Roman law was followed in the construction of this
Edict—and that an acquisition by an onerous title without the intention of
defrauding creditors, or notice of insolvency either direct or constructive,
would have been held valid even if made to a friend of the debtor. Cormier,
who wrote only six years after the promulgation of the Edict of 1609, thus
lays down the law as then understood :

Or, pour y avoir lieu à ceste action (he says) *il faut que le detteur ait
aliener pour frauder ses créanciers ou à la verité, ou par présomption ; et
que celui qui a prins les biens n'ait esté ignorant du conseil et intention
frauduleux.—Ce qui est vray quand on prend la chose en vertu d'un
contract onéreux comme de vendition ou d'eschange ; autrement en serait
si c'estai en vertu de contract lucratif comme de donation ou de legs tes-
tamenta re, car au dit c.s celuy qui a prins sans autre distinction est
tousiours suiet à rendre et restablir, pource qu'il est tousiours desraison-
nables qu'il soit enrichi au dommage des créanciers.* Code Henri IV.,
Liv. 26, col. 1761, No. 5.

In 1667, a *Règlement* was made for the city of Lyons, by which it was
declared that *toutes cessions et transports sur les effects des faillis seront
nuls, s'ils ne sont faits dix jours au moins avant la faillite publiquement
connue.*—Art. 13. By the Ord. of 1673, tit. 11, art. 4, *tous transports, ventes
et donations de biens, meubles ou immeubles, faits en fraude des créanciers,*
were declared null. The former law made a certain proximity to the
period of failure a ground of absolute nullity—without reference to the
intention of the parties—the latter made the fraudulent intention of the
transaction a ground of nullity, without reference to the time at which it
took place. A declaration made in November 1702 extended the *règlement
de Lyon* to the whole kingdom, retaining the 4th article of the Ord. of 1673
in force ; and thereafter if the transaction was within ten days of the failure
no proof of fraud was requisite to annul it ;—if not, it might be annulled by
proving a fraudulent intent. And when such an intent was relied on,
it was necessary to prove the complicity of the person dealing with the
debtor—either directly or constructively—in which proof, the usual pre-
sumptions arising from relationship, the absence or inadequacy of the consideration—and the publicity of the embarrasments of the debtor, would
receive their due weight.

One of the principal difficulties which attended the enforcement of the
declaration of 1702 was the fixation of the date of the failure. The Edict of
1609 and the declaration of 1702, alike described it as being the period at
which the *faillite* became publicly known : *la faillité publiquement connue.*
But this does not in any respect solve the difficulty, except in rare cases; for
while the day of the stoppage of payment by a great commercial house
might be publicly known, the great majority of failures are gradual. In
most of them there is a period of struggle, during which the debtor's difficulties gradually increase, from the first protest or failure to pay—until his
stoppage is entire and irremediable. And it may be as difficult to discover
the date of the first dishonor of a just pecuniary call upon him—as it undoubtedly is to ascertain the moment of time when the continuance of his
business becomes hopeless. In addition to this, unless the insolvent
occupies a prominent position, his failure may never become publicly
known—or known at all, beyond the limited circle of the creditors who
suffer by it.

This difficulty appears scarcely to have received its due weight with the
Commissioners for codifying our laws ; for they suggest articles (Nos. 56 and
59, title of obligations) which would render null all transactions that are
entered into within ten days of the bankruptcy of a trader, without providing

or suggesting any mode in which the date of that bankruptcy can be ascertained or established. And although, in the introductory remarks, a definition of the word bankruptcy is promised—which may remove the difficulty—it is not easy to perceive how a mere definition can reach the evil which it is necessary to guard against.

By the code de commerce of 1808, the transactions of the debtor, preceding the failure, were divided into those which were abso'utely null and those which were surject to be set aside. Under its provi-ions, during the ten days preceding the failure, no privilege or hypotheque could be acquired upon the property of the debtor—no gratuitous transfer of immoveable prop:rty cou'd take p'ace—and no payment of commercial debts, not mature, could be made. All a'ienations, *à titre onereux*, effected during the same period, if appearing to be tainted with fraud, were annullable ; and all commercial engagements contracted by the debtor during that time, were p:esumed to be fraudulent as to him, and were liable to be annulled, on proof of fraud on the part of those in whose favor he contracted them. And, finally, it was declared, as in the old *code marchand*, that *tous faits et payements faits en fraude des créanciers sont nuls.*

But, under this legislation, the difficulty as to the period of failure was again encoun'ered, though in a different form. The *tribunal de commerce* had the power of declaring the period of the *ouverture de la faillite*—and that period was necessarily antecedent to the judgment which establi-hed it. That judgment appeared therefore to be capable of an indirect retroactive operation of an almost unlimited character, upon the previous transactions of the debtor—and in this manner transfers and payments were assailed which had been made many years before the *jugement declaratif de la faillite*, but within ten days of the period to which by such judgment its *ouverture* was referred. In one case, a transfer made seven years before the judgment ; in another, a payment made twenty years before the judgment, were thus attacked—and the inju-tice of such a construction of the law, as was contended for by the plaintiffs in those cases, was so palpable as probably to exercise a con-iderable influence in promoting its rejection. Dalloz Journ. de Cass, 28th May and 22d July, 1823. The decisions of the Court of Cassation, settling the jurispradence upon an equitable basis, by refusing to follow the letter of the Code—was made the subject of much controversy. See Pardessus, Nos. 1119, 1120 and 1121, Hors-un Ques. Nos. 155, 156—Boulay Paty, No. 9 5—2 Renouard, p. 173. But the justice and equity of those decisions, if not their legality, were generally admitted.

By the law of 1838, the provisions of the *code de commerce*, in respect of fraudulent conveyances, was considera'ly changed. The retroact ve character of the judgment declaratory of the failure was mueh mo lified The *dessaisissement* of the debtor reckoned from the date of that judgment, instead of from the date to which that judgment referred the failure. All gratuitous transfers of property, a'l payments of debts not matured, all payments of debts due, made otherwise than in money or in *effets de commerce*—and all securities upon real or personal property, granted for debts previous'y incurred, were declared to be absolutely null, if they occurred within ten days next before the time established by the tribunal as that of the stoppage of payment. And a'l other transacti n- of th debtor, entered into after the stoppage of payment, were annullable, if the party contracting with the debtor knew of such stoppage. No provision is made by it respecting transactions previous to the ten days next before the stoppage, these being left to the operat on of the com non law, as established by art. 1167 of the civil code. And this latter article introduces the rev catory action of the Roman and old French law, for the annu lation of all act- done in fraud of creditors.

In Scotland, the general rule of the c vil law prevails ; but the time, relatively to the Bankruptcy, at which a transac ion takes place has, in certain cases, a direct effect upon the validity of the acts of the Bankrupt Mu doch, pp. 4 to 13. And under that system, as in France and Rome, to annul g a-tuitous alienations by an insolvent, required no proof of fraud on the part of the receiver ; and as it adopts the principle th t, after inso vency, a debtor's property belongs to his creditors ; there is no difference, except in detail, between its provisions on the subject under consideration and those of France.

In England, the intent to defraud creditors, is the only ground required to sustain a demand to annul the debtor's acts. In the English law, such acts are described as being in contemplation of Bankruptcy ; and they are void, as being contrary to the spirit and policy of the Bankrupt law. 1, D. & M., pp. 145 *et seq*. The phrase " in contemplation of Bankruptcy " has, in England, a well-understood technical meaning ; and, as so understoo l, describes with sufficient accuracy the condition of mind of a debtor who makes a fraudulent conveyance or creates a fraudulent preference. A similar phrase is used in our Act , and a reference may be advantageously had to the English authorities for an elucidation of its meaning. See D. & M., *loc : cit :—* Archbold, pp. 307 *et seq.*

It will appear from this cursory examination of the provisions of these different systems of Bankruptcy, on the subject of acts done in fraud of creditors, that their spirit is the same, and that they vary only in detail ; and our own statute has not departed from the principles that have governed the legislation of other countries on the same subject. Under its provisions, as under the laws of ancient Rome, of ancient and modern France, of England and of Scotland, gratuitous alienations of property by an insolvent are invalid ; and all acts are declared to be null which are done by the debtor with intent to defraud, obstruct, impede or delay creditors, if the party contracting with him has actual or constructive notice of the insolvency, and if they serve to defraud, impede or delay creditors. Fraudulent preferences, by securing or paying creditors, to the injury of the estate generally, are declared null ; and if such transactions occur within a time named in the act, they are presumed to have the defects which it pronounces fatal. Consequently, the student of this portion of the act may avail himself of an immense mass of learning, and a vast collection of adjudged cases, to be found in the English, Scotch and French treatises already cited, and in many others ; all of which are as applicable—or nearly so—to our statute as to the systems which they more particularly exemplify.

What shall be deemed fraudulent contracts or conveyances. **8.** All gratuitous contracts or conveyances, or contracts or conveyances without consideration, or with a merely nominal consideration, made by a debtor afterwards becoming an insolvent with or to any person whomsoever, within three months next preceding the date of the assignment or of the issue of the writ of attachment in compulsory liquidation, and all contracts by which creditors are injured, obstructed, or delayed, made by a debtor unable to meet his engagements, and afterwards becoming an insolvent, with a person knowing such inability or having probable cause for believing such inability to exist, or after such inability is public and notorious, are presumed to be made with intent to defraud his creditors :

1. *All gratuitous contracts, or contracts with a merely nominal consideration :--*
ff L. 6, § II. Pothier Oblns.. 153. 3 Nouv. Den. Fraude relativement aux créanciers. § 1, No. 10. Domat liv., 2 tit. 10, sec. 1, No. 6. 6 Toullier, Nos. 353, 354. 3 Bed. du dol, Nos. 1431 et seq. C. com., art. 446. Murdock. pp. 3, 4.

2. *With any person whomsoever—*
As opposed to a person knowing the inability of the debtor to meet his engagements. The gratuitous character of the contract being considered sufficient to establish a presumption of complicity on the part of the recipient of the property. 3 Bed. du dol, No. 1431. Murdoch, p. 3.

3. *Made within three months—*
This period is very long, but as it applies only to gratuitous contracts, it is difficult to see how it can effect any serious injustice to the recipient ; while the creditors whose *gage* the thing conveyed was, will get their rights with regard to it.

4. *By which creditors are injured, obstructed or delayed*—
See authorities above cited, and also 2 Chardon, Nos. 205, 208. **3** Bed.
du dol, No. 1457.

5. *With a person knowing such inability*—
This is in strict conformity with existing law, and with the modern law
of France. Domat, loc. cit., No. 4. Nouv. Pen., loc. cit., Nos. 12, 15. **6**
Toullier, Nos. 348 to 366. 3 Bed. du dol, No. 1432. C. L. art. 1975.

6. *Or after such inability is public and notorious*—
3 Bed. du dol, No. 1439. 2 Chardon, No. 208.

7. *Are presumed to be made with intent*—
No evidence is required to establish the intent, the presumption created
by the circumstances being sufficient.
The consequence of such a presumption arising, are shewn in p. 3, *post.*

2. A contract or conveyance for consideration by which Contracts or
creditors are injured or obstructed, made by a debtor unable to conveyances
meet his engagements with a person ignorant of such inability, made by in-
solvent void-
and before it has become public and notorious, but within able in certain
thirty days next before the execution of a deed of assignment cases.
or of a writ of attachment under this Act, is voidable, and may
be set aside by any Court of competent jurisdiction, upon such
terms as to the protection of such person from actual loss or
liability by reason of such contract, as the Court may order;

1. *With a person ignorant of such inability*—
This ignorance is insufficient to protect the recipient of the insolvent's
property, if the contract or conveyance injures or obstructs the creditors, and
if it be made within thirty days of the insolvency. But in consideration of
the good faith of the party contracting with the insolvent, such a contract is
not absolutely void, but only voidable, and may be rescinded upon conditions
which will protect him from injury.

2. *Upon such terms as to the protection*—
If a deed be rescinded on the ground that it was executed in fraud of
creditors, the consideration actually given would have to be ranked for as
a common debt, by the party who gave it In the case under consideration,
the Court would probably order the repayment of such consideration as a
condition precedent to the recovery of the property. And many similar
cases may be imagined, where the power thus conferred upon the Court
would have a just and beneficial operation.

3. *Actual loss or liability*—
These expressions do not seem to convey any right to indemnity for
damages to the party ousted.

3. All contracts or conveyances made and acts done by a Fraudulent
debtor, with intent fraudulently to impede, obstruct, or delay contracts or
conveyances
his creditors in their remedies against him, or with intent to by insolvent
defraud his creditors, or any of them, and so made, done, and void.
intended with the knowledge of the person contracting or acting
with the debtor, and which have the effect of impeding, obs-
tructing, or delaying the creditors in their remedies, or of inju-
ring them, or any of them, are prohibited, and are null and
void, notwithstanding that such contracts, conveyances, or acts
be in consideration or in contemplation of marriage ;

1. *All contracts or conveyances* * • • *with intent*—
All such transactions as are described in this clause have been null
under the law of France for centuries—and they were so also under the
Roman law. *ff* L. 1, §§ 1 and 2. Quæ in fraudem credit.—Edit. de Henri

IV., 1609. Règlement pour la Ville de Lyon, 1667. Ord. 1673, Tit. 11, art. 4. Ord. de 1679. Déclaration de 1702. Pothier Oblns., No. 153. Nouv. Den., Fraude relt. aux créanciers, § 1, No. 10. Domat loc. cit. 6 Toullier loc. cit. 3 Bed. du dol, No. 1428.

2. *With the knowledge of the person contracting*—
The person contracting with the debtor must be aware of the debtor's intent, or the contract is valid. Joussé sur l'Ord., 1673, tit. 11, art. 4. 3 Bed. du dol, No. 1432.

But this knowledge will be presumed in the case of gratuitous contracts—*conveyances à vil prix*—the notorious insolvency of the debtor and the like. See note to p. 1, *ante.*

3. *And which have the effect*—
There must always be the *eventus damni*, as well as the *consilium fraudis.*

In what case preferential sales, &c., shall be deemed fraudulent.

4. If any sale, deposit, pledge, or transfer, be made by any person in contemplation of insolvency, by way of security for payment to any creditor, or if any goods, effects, or valuable security be given by way of payment by such person to any creditor, whereby such creditor obtains or will obtain an unjust preference over the other creditors, such sale, deposit, pledge, transfer, or payment, shall be null and void, and the subject thereof may be recovered back for the benefit of the estate by the assignee, in any Court of competent jurisdiction ; and if the same be made within thirty days next before the execution of a deed of assignment, or the issue of a writ of attachment under this Act, it shall be presumed to have been so made in contemplation of insolvency ;

1. *In contemplation of insolvency*—
And, therefore, if by any such transaction the creditor obtains, or will obtain, a peference over other creditors, it will be null. See introductory note to this §, *ante.*

The phrase " in contemplation of insolvency " does not mean in contemplation of the issue of a writ, nor of the execution of a deed of assignment, but merely that the debtor is conscious of being in difficulty, and of the probability of insolvency occurring ; and gives the security or makes the payment as a precaution against insolvency. As has already been stated, this phrase is used in the English Act, and there have been numerous expressions of opinion by the English Judges upon its true meaning. Bayley, J., (Gibbins vs. Phillips, 7 B. and C., 534,) says, that it would be sufficient to establish the contemplation of bankruptcy if the debtor knew himself to be in such a situation that he must be supposed to have anticipated that in all human probability a bankruptcy must follow ; and he adds, that in this sense, contemplation of bankruptcy has always been considered evidence of fraud, although the party may not have expected the actual and immediate issue of a commission. And afterwards in Poland vs. Glyn, reported *in notis*, 4 Bing. 22, Abbott, C. J., told the jury, that the object of the bankrupt laws being to divide the whole of the bankrupt's property equally amongst his creditors ; if a tradesman found himself in such a situation, that in the judgment of any reasonable man a bankruptcy was inevitable, no voluntary payment by him could be good, and Justices Bayley, Holroyd and Best afterwards concurred in his view of the subject. And Wilde, C. J., in Brown vs. Kempton. 13 L. T., Rep. 11, states the rule still more clearly. He says in this case, " that if a payment were made at a time when the bankrupts had a view to bankruptcy, though they might hope to avoid bankruptcy, yet if made with the object of giving the creditor an eventual advantage, if the bankruptcy did take place, the payment was illegal and invalid."

These *dicta*, not only aid in construing the expression used in this clause, but fairly describe the position of a debtor, and the effect of his acts under our own law, when he has really ceased to possess sufficient assets to meet his liabilities, and when he has become aware of the fact. The equitable provisions of that law, make the property of the insolvent debtor the *gage* of his creditors, and direct its apportionment among them, according to the amounts of their claims. And any act of the insolvent debtor tending to disturb this equality, will be annulled by the Court. See the authorities already cited, and also Rep. de Guyot vo. *Déconfiture, Banqueroute.* 2 Chardon, 389, 393, 407. Capmas, pp. 76-81. Bryson, vs. Dickson, 3 L. C. Rep., p. 65. Sharing vs. Meunier, 7 L. C. Rep., p. 250. Cumming vs. Mann, 2 L. C. Jur., 195. Cumming vs. Smith, 5 L. C. Jur., p. 1. Macfarlane vs. McKenzie, 5 L. C. Jur., p. 109. Duncan vs. Wilson et al., 2 L. C. Jur., 253. Withall & Young & Michon, 10 L. C. Rep., 149. 10 Louisiana, p. 605. Civil Code of L. C. Obligations, Nos. 51 to 60.

The rule, however, must not be extended too far, by applying it to cases in which the giving of security is not prompted by the anticipation or expectation of insolvency, but is merely the result of an ordinary and business-like arrangement beween the parties. Most security is probably taken as a precaution against insolvency, and in that sense may be said to be so given in contemplation of it ; but no system of bankruptcy law goes the length of invalidating such securities. The law does not seek to impugn the contract by which the debtor, for a valuable consideration ; such as an extension of time, a reduction of interest or the like ; endeavors to protect his creditor from the general and ordinary contingencies of a commercial career; but assails such transactions only when their object is to protect the creditor from a specific, visible and impending danger.

2. *By way of security—or by way of payment—*
The class of transactions referred to in this clause, consists only of those by which the position of a creditor is improved, or is intended to be improved, at the expense of his fellow creditors. No doubt the giving of security to a creditor, or of effects other than mere money as payment, might be held to fall within the general terms of the last two preceding clauses of this section ; but the species of commercial fraud against which this clause is intended to guard, is so prevalent, and its perpetration generally so easy, that it appears to have been thought necessary to provide still more specifically against it. Its peculiar characteristic is the fact of a pre-existing debt, for which security is given subsequent to its creation, or which is paid otherwise than in money, when the debtor sees a probability of his estate falling into insolvency, and desires to prevent loss to the creditor in such an event. And the evil it seeks to prevent, is the deterioration of the estate by preferences to creditors who have become so on the same terms as others, but who from one motive or another, when the danger of insolvency becomes imminent ; are protected by the debtor out of the assets of his estate, which all his creditors are entitled to regard as their common security.

3. *Creditor obtains, or will obtain, an unjust preference—*
The knowledge of the creditor is not made essential to the invalidity of the transaction, nor is the time of it relatively to the insolvency, of any importance as matter of law ; and in this respect this clause differs from all the other clauses of this chapter. The reasons undoubtedly are that the creditor who seeks to change his position, after it has been deliberately taken, must be presumed to have some reason for doing so, which has been suggested by facts that have fallen within his knowledge : and facts which cause him to fear the non-payment of his debt, can only be such facts as warn him of difficulty, and of threatening, if not actually approaching insolvency. If under these circumstances, the debtor, conscious of impending failure, yields to a demand for protection against it, or even voluntarily provides such protection to his creditor, there is really a concurrence of intention on both sides to diminish the mass of the assets, for the benefit of one creditor and to the injury of the others. And the circumstances which must be presumed to have arisen, to cause the creditor to demand or even to accept further security for his debt, are also presumed

to be a warning to him that the taking of such further security is illegal and improper, and thereby to constitute him an accomplice in the fraud committed by the debtor in giving it to him. Bed., Nos. 113 et seq. And this rule is far from being purely modern, for we find M. Cormier stating in 1615, with reference to the Paulian action : " *icelle mesme action se donne contre celuy qui sçachant son detteur n'estre solvable tire et retorque quelque chose de luy par quelque contract que ce soit, comme de vendition, d'engagement, de dation, ou constitution ou acceptilation, ou par quelque autre paction.*" Code Henri IV., Liv. 26, Col. 1762, No. 10.

When payments shall be deemed fraudulent.

Proviso.

5. Every payment made within thirty days next before the execution of a deed of assignment, or the issue of a writ of attachment under this Act, by a debtor unable to meet his engagements in full, to a person knowing such inability, or having probable cause for believing the same to exist, is void, and the amount paid may be recovered back by suit, in any competent Court, for the benefit of the estate ; Provided always, that if any valuable security be given up in consideration of such payment, such security or the value thereof, shall be restored to the creditor before the return of such payment can be demanded ;

1. *Payment made within thirty days—*
This means a payment in money, as the last previous clause provided the rule with regard to payments effected by means of the transfer of effects or valuable securities ; and it does not seem to be intended that any payment made previous to the thirty days antecedent to the insolvency should be enquired into at all.
The Code of 1808 was more stringent with regard to payments ; for while it declared null all payments of debts not exigible, made during the ten days preceding the failure—Art. 446—it also declared null, without reference to time, all payments made in fraud of creditors.—Art. 447.
The Code of 1838, softened very much the rigor of that of 1808 in this respect. Under its provisions, as under those of the former, all payments of non-exigible debts, made within ten days of the stoppage of payment, are null : and payments made within the same period—in effects other than money or negotiable paper—of debts exigible are also void. Art. 446. 1 Bed., faillites, Nos. 110 et seq. But there is no provision prohibiting payment in money or bills at any time previous to the stoppage of payment ; nor any rule rendering any such payment liable to be enquired into.—A similar principle prevailed under the *regime* of the Ord. of 1673, Jousse, pp. 156 et seq. Savary, Parères, No. 39, p. 311. For the English rules on the subject of payments by the bankrupt, see 1 D. & M., pp. 457 et seq.
2. *To a person knowing—or having probable cause for believing—*
These circumstances have always been held to make the person dealing with the insolvent a constructive participant in the fraud. 2 Chardon, p. 373, No. 208. Nouv. Den. vo. Fraude. 2 Horson, Quest. 155, p. 283. See also Code Louis. art. 1979. 10 Louis. Rep. 605.

Transfer of debts due by insolvent, to be void in certain cases.

6. Any transfer of a debt due by the insolvent, made within thirty days next previous to the execution of a deed of assignment or the issue of a writ of attachment under this Act, or at any time afterwards, to a debtor knowing or having probable cause for believing the Insolvent to be unable to meet his engagements, or in contemplation of his insolvency, for the purpose of enabling the debtor to set up by way of compensation or set-off the debt so transferred, is null and void as regards the estate of the Insolvent ; and the debt due to the

estate of the Insolvent shall not be compensated or affected in any manner by a claim so acquired ; but the purchaser thereof may rank on the estate in the place and stead of the original creditor ;

Any transfer—
That is a transfer of a debt due by the insolvent, obtained by one who is indebted to him ; and who knows him to be, or believes that he is about to become, insolvent, for the purpose of being set off or pleaded in compensation of the debt so due to the insolvent's estate. Such a transaction though not participated in by the debtor, or even known to him, is a fraud upon his creditors ; as it appropriates an asset of the estate to the payment of one of its liabilities, as effectually as if the insolvent had himself handed over to his debtor a part of his property wherewith to pay the debt.
The same rule prevailed in France. 1 Bed., faillites, Nos. 113 to 116 *bis.*

7. Any trader in Lower Canada, and any person whosoever in Upper Canada, who purchases goods on credit or procures advances in money, knowing or believing himself to be unable to meet his engagements, and concealing the fact from the person thereby becoming his creditor, with the intent to defraud such person, or who by any false pretence obtains a term of credit for the payment of any advance or loan of money, or of the price or any part of the price of any goods, wares or merchandize, with intent to defraud the person thereby becoming his creditor, and who shall not afterwards have paid the debt or debts so incurred, shall be held to be guilty of a fraud, and shall be liable to imprisonment for such time as the Court may order, not exceeding two years, unless the debt or costs be sooner paid ; and if such debt or debts be incurred by a trading company, then every member thereof who shall not prove himself to have been ignorant of the incurring, and of the intention to incur, such debt or debts, shall be similarly liable ; provided always, that in the suit or proceeding taken for the recovery of such debt or debts, the defendant be charged with such fraud, and be declared to be guilty of it by the judgment rendered in such suit or proceeding ; *(margin: Certain other frauds defined, as regards L. C.) (Punishment.) (Proviso.)*

1· *Any trader in Lower Canada and any person whomsoever in Upper Canada—*
There does not seem to be any good reason for this distinction—as the offence created by this clause has no relation to the proceedings for winding up the estate of the debtor and for enabling him to obtain a discharge from his liabilities, which form the principal objects of the law. The clause originally applied only to traders, and the distinction between Upper and Lower Canada must have been created without due consideration, when the operation of the Bill generally, was extended to all classes in Upper Canada.
2. *Concealing the fact—*
That is not informing him of the fact. Active proceedings for its concealment could hardly be considered necessary.
3. *With intent to defraud—*
Actor non facit reum nisi mens sit rea. 3 Inst., 307. The intent and the act must both concur to constitute the offence. Per Lord Kenyon, 7 T. R., 514. And the intent must exist at the time the purchase was made, or the advance obtained. Reg. vs. Wood, 1 Denison, C. C. 387. Reg. vs. Preston, 2 Denison, C. C. 353.

But the intent could doubtless be inferred from the position and conduct of the accused ; without direct evidence of it. See the cases collected as to intent to defraud, in Roscoe's Criminal evidence, p. 418.

4. *Who shall not afterwards have paid—*

As the proceeding contemplated by this clause—and the remedy it gives, are rather civil than criminal—and rather intended to enforce payment than to punish the debtor; he may relieve himself from them by paying the debt.

5. *Unless the debt and costs be sooner paid—*

See last note.

6. *Every member thereof who shall not prove himself to be ignorant of—*

That is to say, that after the fraudulent act has been brought home to one of the partners, the burden of proof as to the complicity or innocence of the others is shifted upon them. This would seem harsh, but the law applies only to cases where the debt is incurred on behalf of the partnership, and where a presumption therefore fairly arises against the partners, as having profited by the transaction.

7. *That in the suit or proceeding—the defendant be charged with the fraud—*

This requires specific allegations to be made in the declaration, charging the defendant with the fraud; and in Lower Canada, an appropriate conclusion also, demanding a judicial declaration of guilt, and the condemnation of the accused to the term of imprisonment considered adequate to the circumstances.

As to like case in U. C. 8. In Upper Canada in every such suit or proceeding whether the defendant appears and pleads, or makes default, the plaintiff shall be bound to prove the fraud charged, and upon his proving it the Judge who tries the suit or proceeding shall immediately after the verdict rendered against the defendant for such fraud (if such verdict is given) adjudge the term of imprisonment which the defendant shall undergo ; and he shall forthwith order and direct the defendant immediately to be taken into custody and imprisoned accordingly ; but such judgment shall not affect the ordinary remedies for the revision thereof, or of any proceeding in the case.

Appears and pleads or makes default—
This provision is probably intended to prevent a Judgment from being entered up without proof, on the mere default of the defendant to appear—which cannot be done in Lower Canada.

OF COMPOSITION AND DISCHARGE.

When and to what extent a deed of composition shall be binding. 9. A deed of composition and discharge executed by the majority in number, of those of the creditors of an Insolvent who are respectively creditors for sums of one hundred dollars and upwards, and who represent at least three-fourths in value of the liabilities of the Insolvent subject to be computed in ascertaining such proportion, shall have the same effect with regard to the remainder of his creditors, and be binding to the same extent upon him, and upon them, as if they were also parties to it ; and such a deed may be validly made either **When such deed may be made.** before, pending, or after proceedings upon an assignment, or for the compulsory liquidation of the estate of the insolvent ; and the discharge therein agreed to shall have the same effect as an ordinary discharge obtained as hereinafter provided :

1. *Majority in number of creditors for sums of* $100 *and upwards*—
In calculating this majority, those creditors whose claims are not extinguished by an ordinary discharge obtained under the Act—and privileged creditors - are not counted in any way ; unless the first mentioned class consent, in which case they may be.—See p. 5. *post.*

2. *Three fourths in value of the liabilities*—
This is not limited to the value of the liabilities amounting to $100 and upwards, and therefore must include all the liabilities of the Insolvent, subject to the exceptions referred to in the next note. There is a discrepancy in different parts of the Act, in the mode of stating the proportion in value of the creditors which is required to give validity to their acts. In §3 p. 19, for instance, the power is granted to " the majority in number, and three fourths in value of the creditors for sums above one hundred dollars," in which case the amount due to creditors in sums of $100 and less, would not count either as to number or value. And the general rule as to meetings of creditors, gives the controlling power to " the majority in number of all creditors for sums above one hundred dollars * * * representing also the majority in value of *such* creditors: " thus excluding creditors of sums of $100 or less, from being computed as to number or value.—§ 11, p. 2. Those distinctions, though probably not intended, must not be lost sight of by the practitioner.

3. *Subject to be computed* —
For debts which are not subject to be computed, see p. 5, *post.*

4. *Upon him*—
The most important point in which a deed of this description is binding upon a debtor, is the payment of the composition agreed upon ; and under this clause, a creditor who is not a party to the deed, will have the same remedies for enforcing such payment, as one who has executed it.

5. *May be validly made either before, pending, or after*—
Although this clause establishes that such a deed may be validly *made*— it is important to consider what effect it will have, previous to the expiration of the two months which are allowed to creditors for filing their claims.

The spirit of the law appears to be, to allow a delay of two months after the appointment of an assignee—within which claims are to be filed— foreign creditors will have time to come in,—and the assignee may be supposed to have acquired a knowledge of the estate, sufficient to enable him to scrutinise the claims made. It would appear to be the intention of the Act that until this period expires, the creditors do not acquire that entire control of the estate which they may afterwards exercise. Until then dividends cannot be declared, § 5, p. 1 ; the meeting for the public examination of the Bankrupt cannot be held, § 10, p. 1 ; the creditors cannot act in the removal of the assignee, § 4, p. 18 ; and they cannot pass resolutions on the various subjects respecting which authority is given them—without special notice, except at the first meeting held after this period, § 11, p. 3. The reasons for the adoption of these rules doubtless are, that the actual creditors and amount of indebtedness cannot sooner be ascertained with any approach to certainty ; that the creditors as a body cannot be expected to be sooner prepared to assert their rights in the estate with advantage ; and that a knowledge of the indebtedness of the insolvent, and the co-operation of his creditors, are both required, in acting upon the more important provisions of the law.

The effect of a composition deed depends entirely upon the number and amount of the creditors who sign it—and therefore as much as any other matter or proceeding contemplated by the Act, requires an exact knowledge of the amount due by the insolvent, and of the creditors who represent that amount. And since this knowledge cannot be fully attained until after the period of two months allowed for the filing of claims ; the insolvent claiming protection under a deed of composition and discharge, before the expiration of that period ; or before his estate has been brought within the operation of the Act at all ; must find it difficult, or impossible, to shew that the proportion of creditors in number and value required to give it validity, have concurred in it.

Again, by p. 2, post—the insolvent is permitted to deposit a deed of composition and discharge, with the assignee—who may thereupon take steps to divest himself of the estate. But he cannot take the initiative towards this object in the smallest particular, until after the expiry of the two months. If the deed can be held to establish his discharge before the expiry of the two months, he should receive back his estate at the time his discharge is so established. If the deed has acquired its full validity, the creditors have no claim to the estate. If, on the other hand, the deed does not receive its full effect until after the expiry of the two months has furnished the assignee and any dissenting creditors, with the means of knowing whether it is entitled to any weight or not—the provision delaying the delivery back of the estate till after that period is consistent with the construction of the Act, which would delay the effect of the discharge to the same extent.

Again, the first clause provides that the discharge agreed to in a deed of composition and discharge, shall have the same effect as an ordinary discharge obtained as thereinafter provided. By p. 3, *post*, the effect of an ordinary discharge is described, and it will be found to operate upon debts and liabilities, for a full discovery of which the two months delay is requisite.

Upon these considerations, it would seem to be a reasonable construction of this clause, to hold that a deed of composition and discharge will not operate effectually the discharge of the debtor ; or perhaps it would be more correct to say, will not be susceptible of being effectually used as establishing a discharge, until after the expiration of the period of two months from the public notice of the appointment of an assignee.

This construction does not by any means deprive the clause under consideration of a character of great importance to the debtor. The procuring the consent of creditors to a deed of composition and discharge, is generally a work of time ; and this clause permits that work to be proceeded with while proceedings in insolvency are maturing, and even before they have commenced. So that when the time arrives at which under p. 2, the assignee may give notice of the deposit of the deed, the insolvent may have already procured its execution in .readiness for such deposit. And there seems to be no reason why the application for confirmation should not also be proceeding, provided the debtor is confident that he has succeeded in obtaining the assent to it of the requisite proportion of his creditors.

6. *The same effect as an ordinary discharge—*
See *post*, p. 3.

Notice and
time within
which opposi-
tion to com-
position must
be made.

If none be so
made.

2. If the Insolvent procures a deed of composition and discharge to be duly executed as aforesaid, and deposits it with the assignee pending the proceedings upon a voluntary assignment or for compulsory liquidation, the assignee, after the period hereinbefore fixed as that after which dividends may be declared has elapsed, shall give notice of such deposit by advertisement ; and if opposition to such composition and discharge be not made by a creditor, within six juridical days after the last publication of such notice, by filing with the assignee a declaration in writing that he objects to such composition and discharge, the assignee shall act upon such deed of composition and discharge according to its terms; but if opposition be made thereto within the said period, or if made be not withdrawn, then he shall abstain from taking any action upon such deed until the same has been confirmed, as hereinafter provided ;

1. *Period at which dividends may be declared—*
That is two months from the first insertion of the advertisement giving notice of the appointment of an assignee. § 5, p. 1.

2. *Shall act upon such deed—*

If by the deed it is agreed that the debtor shall have immediate possession of his estate, the assignee should deliver it over to him. And so with
any other provision contained in the deed, which falls within the province
of the assignee to carry out. It will therefore be necessary in preparing
such a deed to make provision respecting everything required to be done.
Such, for instance, as the payment of such charges as the assignee may
lawfully make, or may be bound to make good ; the assumption by the
debtor of pending suits ; the transfer to him of amounts due the assignee for
sales made, and every other matter or thing, the omission to provide for
which could cause embarrassment, in obtaining back the estate.

If it should afterwards happen that the discharge contained in a deed of
composition is annulled by the Court, a question may arise as to the position
of the estate in that event, supposing it to have been returned to the debtor
by the assignee. There is no express provision on this point in the Act,
but probably the assignee would be entitled to revendicate the property
belonging to the estate ; or in cases of compulsory liquidation, to obtain the
issue of an *alias* or further writ of attachment in the original cause, by a
petition founded upon affidavit. The case is not likely to occur, as any
creditor having objections to make, would file them in the manner provided
for by this section, and thus prevent the estate from passing out of the
hands of the assignee.

3. *Has been confirmed—*

Under ps. **6** and **8** *post.*

3. The consent in writing of the said proportion of creditors
to the discharge of a debtor after an assignment, or after his
estate has been put in compulsory liquidation, absolutely frees
and discharges him from all liabilities whatsoever (except such
as are hereinafter specially excepted) existing against him and
proveable against his estate, which are mentioned and set forth
in the statement of his affairs annexed to the deed of assignment, or which are shewn by any supplementary list of
creditors furnished by the insolvent, previous to such discharge,
and in time to permit the creditors therein mentioned obtaining
the same dividend as other creditors upon his estate, or which
appear by any claim subsequently furnished to the assignee,
whether such debts be exigible or not at the time of his insolvency, and whether direct or indirect ; and if the holder of any
negotiable paper is unknown to the insolvent, the insertion of
the particulars of such paper in such statement of affairs, with
the declaration that the holder thereof is unknown to him, shall
bring the debt represented by such paper, and the holder
thereof, within the operation of this section ; *Effect of consent of credi-
tors to debt-
or's discharge.*

*If the holder
of any nego-
tiable paper
is unknown.*

1. *Absolutely frees and discharges him from all liabilities—*

There are exceptions to this discharge which are referred to in the
remainder of this clause, but they do not interfere with the principle of the
general rule, that by a discharge under this Act, the insolvent is freed from
all debts and claims whatsoever. Notwithstanding the apparent compre-
hensiveness of the phraseology of this clause, the question is frequently
asked whether liabilities incurred previous to the passage of the Act, are
discharged, or only those subsequent to its enactment—in other words,
whether the Act is retrospective or not.

It must be admitted that in general, the idea of a law which has a retrospective character is repugnant to a strict sense of justice. And although
the right of the Legislature to pass such laws cannot be denied, their terms
will be strictly scrutinised and construed. And a retroactive effect will not

be conceded to them, unless those terms unmistakeably convey it. To deal with the latter proposition first, and ascertain whether or no the terms of this Act unmistakeably confer upon it a retrospective character, it will only be necessary cursorily to refer to a few of the clauses bearing upon the question.

The preamble declares it to be "expedient that provision be made for the settlement of the estates of insolvent debtors." This phrase clearly covers debtors then insolvent, by its natural grammatical meaning ; for if it intended only those who should thereafter become insolvent, it would have been necessary to adopt an entirely different form of words.

The same remark will apply to the form of words used in § 2, p. 1. The words "any person unable to meet his engagements," according to their ordinary grammatical meaning, would strictly apply only to those persons who were unable to meet their engagements at the time the act was passed, or, perhaps, at the time it came into force ; but, as the law is regarded as always speaking, it comprehends also all those who shall subsequently labor under the disability indicated.

Under these clauses, therefore, a person who became insolvent before the act passed, and remained insolvent when it came into operation, is subject to its provisions.

Again, the enactments respecting compulsory liquidation, all contemplate the machinery of the law being susceptible of being set in motion immediately upon the law coming into force. If the debtor committed any one of the numerous acts of insolvency described in the act, on the 2nd September last, he could have been forthwith dispossessed of his estate, and the proceedings for that purpose could have been instituted by "any creditor." See § 3, *passim*. It is plain that in this case also the words "any creditor" cannot, by any recognized rule of construction, be held to mean those creditors only whose claims arose upon or after the 1st September last.

The debts which are entitled to be proved against the estate, are, "all debts due and payable at the time of the execution of the deed of assignment, or at the time of the issue of a writ of attachment, &c., &c. § 5, p. 2. In this provision, debts which arose previous to the passing of the act are unmistakeably comprised.

The estate which passes to the assignee is, all the property of the debtor, real and personal, "which he has or may become entitled to at any time before his discharge is effected."—§ 2 p. 7 ; § 3. p. 22. So that there can be no doubt but that it is a matter of perfect indifference, whether he acquired such property before or after the passage of the act.

And, lastly, the clause now under consideration expressly declares, that the consent of the requisite proportion of creditors absolutely frees and discharges the Insolvent from " all liabilities whatsoever existing against him, and proveable against his estate." Here, again, it is impossible to deny that the phrase "all liabilities whatsoever *existing* against him," must comprise every such liability, without reference to the period of its inception.

This statute, therefore, is retroactive, and to such an extent, that persons who became insolvent previous to its passage fall within its provisions ; that persons who acquired the quality of creditors before it passed, may avail themselves of the proceedings it authorizes ; that the debts due to those creditors may rank upon the estate of the insolvent ; that property acquired by him before it became law, becomes vested in his assignee under its provisions ; and, finally, that by a discharge under this act he is freed from the liabilities he incurred before it was enacted.

Whatever may be the general principles applicable to retrospective legislation, and however strong may be the feeling against giving retroactivity to statutes, it may reasonably be asserted that the nature and purposes of a Bankrupt or Insolvent law, necessarily exclude it from the operation of those principles, and prevent its being obnoxious to the objections usually urged against retroactive laws. And in fact that a Bankrupt or Insolvent law having exclusively a prospective effect, must necessarily be partial and unjust. This latter proposition, which includes the former, cannot be better sustained than by quoting from an admirable little treatise published in 1843, on the retroactivity of the Bankrupt Ordinance, 2 Vict., cap. 36, and of Bankrupt laws in general, attributed to the present Mr. Justice Meredith :

" In order " (it is said at page 20,) " to effect that which is the primary object of every Bankrupt law, that is, to secure the whole of the bankrupt estate for the benefit of all the creditors, it is absolutely necessary to deprive the debtor of all his ordinary rights over his property. The assignment by the Commissioners has this effect, and the warrant in bankruptcy absolutely prevents the debtor from paying any of his creditors. The debtor being thus by a single blow, denuded of all his property for the benefit of all his creditors, it would be manifestly unjust to allow a part of the creditors to administer and divide his estate according to their own interests and wishes ; and at the same time to permit the remainder of the creditors to harass the debtor with executions and imprisonment ; yet such must be the result if we confine the Bankrupt law to a merely prospective operation.

" The creditors whose debts had been contracted after the passing of the Bankrupt law, would, of course, avail themselves of the advantages which it affords them, and place themselves in immediate possession of the whole of the bankrupt's property ; and the creditors, whose debts date before the passing of the law, by refraining to come in under the commission, would have it in their power to harass the debtor, thus divested of all means of satisfying their claims.

" So long as the debtor has his estate in his own hands, he need not despair ; his friends, to supply a deficiency, may come to his assistance ; his creditors may accept a compromise, or he may by some fortunate speculation increase his means, so as to meet the demands of his creditors ; but no situation in life can be more utterly hopeless, or more deserving of commiseration than that of an honest debtor, who, after having been divested by law of every vestige of his property, is cast upon the world, destitute of all means, and still exposed to the claims of unrelenting creditors.

" A system of law which would thus on the one hand deprive the debtor of his property, and prohibit him from paying any of his creditors, and which at the same time would allow some of those creditors to coerce his person for the purpose of obtaining payment from him, would be in the last degree tyrannical and unjust.

" Every humane or just mind must admit, that the same law which prohibits the debtor from paying any one of his creditors, ought to prevent every one of his creditors from suing him ; that if the creditors, contrary to common law, are allowed to enter upon the estate of the debtor, and manage it as they wish, without reference to the interests of the debtor, they cannot complain if obliged to content themselves with that estate ; in short, that the law which deprives an honest man of all his assets, should at the same time relieve him from all his liabilities."

Probably enough has been said to establish that the present Act is retroactive in its operation, in so far as regards the distribution of the assets of the insolvent among his creditors and his discharge, and that it is just that it should have such operation. But if a more full examination of the general question be desired, see the pamphlet referred to, where the subject of the retroactivity of Bankrupt laws is clearly and carefully treated.

2. *Which are mentioned and set forth—*

This clause describes the debts from which the debtor is freed by a discharge under the Act. They appear to be the following :

a. All debts mentioned in the statement annexed to the deed of assignment ;

b. All debts mentioned in any supplementary statement furnished by him previous to the discharge, in time to have a dividend reserved upon them ;

c. All debts which appear by any claim filed ;

d. All debts upon negotiable paper mentioned by him in his statements the holders being unknown.

It may be stated in general terms that the debtor is discharged from all debts, the existence of which is disclosed by him or by the creditors themselves. The object of this provision evidently is to hold out the strongest possible inducement to the debtor to give full particulars of his liabilities ;

5

and as the neglect of this duty imperils his discharge, the greatest care should always be taken 'by the insolvent to include in his statements every debt that can be alleged to exist against him. In doing this, it is not necessary to admit the whole of a debt to be due, if in reality its amount is disputed. It can be mentioned in the statement according to the amount claimed—and either simply described as " disputed," or a more particular description may be inserted of the grounds of objection to it. And in cases of compulsory liquidation, the debtor should see that every creditor has filed his claim—and if not, should produce and file a list of liabilities shewing those who have not done so. For unless this precaution be taken, a creditor may retain his recourse against the debtor simply by abstaining from fyling his claim. See for the effect of a discharge 1 D & M. p. 734, and as to questions arising upon debts contracted in a foreign country, see Story on conflict of laws, pp. 567 *et seq.*

3. *Obtaining the same dividend—*

Any time before the final dividend will do, because a creditor who had not previously proved, would be entitled to be collocated in the final dividend sheet for all previous dividends out of the moneys in hand, before those who had received the previous dividends could get anything.

4. *Unknown to the Insolvent—*

See § 2, p. 2

Effect of discharge as regards persons as secondarily liable for debts of insolvent.

4. A discharge under this Act shall not operate any change in the liability of any person or company secondarily liable for the debts of the insolvent, either as drawer or endorser of negotiable paper, or as guarantor, surety or otherwise, nor of any partner or other person liable jointly or severally with the insolvent for any debt, nor shall it affect any mortgage, *hypothèque,* lien or collateral security held by any creditor as security for any debt thereby discharged ;

Shall not operate any change—

The object of this clause is to protect the creditor to whom the bankrupt is primarily liable, from losing his recourse against endorsers or sureties by consenting to his discharge. A similar provision is to be found in the Scotch Act, § 56. Murdoch, p. 225. See as to English rule, Brown vs. Carr. 7 Bing., 508. Ex parte Williamson. 1 Atk., 84. Taylor vs. Mills. 2 Cowp., 525. Young vs. Hochley. 3 Wils., 346. Inglis vs. Macdougal. 1 Moore, 196. See also Code Com., art., 545. 2 Bedarride, p. 499.

Certain debts excepted from operation of discharge.

5. A discharge under this Act shall not apply, without the express consent of the creditor, to any debt for enforcing the payment of which the imprisonment of the debtor is permitted by this Act, nor to any debt due as damages for personal wrongs, or as a penalty for any offence of which the insolvent has been convicted, or as a balance of account due by the insolvent as an assignee, tutor, curator, trustee, executor or public officer ; nor shall such debts, nor any privileged debts, nor the creditors thereof, be computed in ascertaining whether a sufficient proportion of the creditors of the insolvent have done, or consented to any act, matter or thing under this Act ; but the creditor of any debt due as a balance of account by the insolvent as assignee, tutor, curator, trustee, executor or public officer, may claim and accept a dividend thereon from the estate without being in any respect affected by any discharge obtained by the insolvent ;

But the creditor may accept the dividend.

1. *Be computed—*
For instance, if a debtor owed £9,000, of which £500 was a balance of amount due by him as tutor, and £500 due as arrears of salary, not in any case exceeding three months, to his clerks and *employés,* he would not be relieved from a demand of payment of such balance of account, or by any discharge under the Act, unless the creditor of it consented to the discharge. If therefore such creditor refused to consent, £6,000 would be a sufficient proportion-in value to render his discharge valid as to ordinary claims. If such creditor consented, the debtor would require the consent of creditors representing £6,375 currency, to constitute such proportion. For in the one case neither the balance of account nor the privileged claims would form part of the mass, in the other, the balance of account would form part of it, but not the privileged debt.

6. An insolvent who has procured a consent to his discharge or the execution of a deed of composition and discharge, within the meaning of this Act, may file in the office of the court the consent or deed of composition and discharge, and may then give notice (Form O.) of the same being so filed, and of his intention to apply by petition to the Court in Lower Canada, or in Upper Canada to the Judge, on a day named in such notice, for a confirmation of the discharge effected thereby ; and notice shall be given by advertisement in the *Canada Gazette* for two months, and also for the same period, if the application is to be made in Upper Canada, in one newspaper, and if in Lower Canada in one newspaper published in French, and in one newspaper published in English, in or nearest the place of residence of the insolvent ; and upon such application, any creditor of the insolvent may appear and oppose such confirmation, either upon the ground of fraud or fraudulent preference within the meaning of this Act, or of fraud or evil practice in procuring the consent of the creditors to the discharge, or their execution of the deed of composition and discharge, as the case may be, or of the insufficiency in number or value of the creditors consenting to or executing the same, or of the fraudulent retention and concealment by the insolvent of some portion of his estate or effects, or of the evasion, prevarication or false swearing of the insolvent upon examination as to his estate and effects, or upon the ground that subsequent to the passing of this Act the insolvent has not kept an account-book shewing his receipts and disbursements of cash, and such other books of account as are suitable for his trade, or if, having at any time kept such book or books, he has refused to produce or deliver them to the assignee ;

Proceedings to obtain confirmation of discharge.

Creditors may oppose, and on what grounds.

1. *Of his intention to apply—*
Notice of this application may be given at any time after the assignee has been appointed, if the insolvent has procured the requisite consent, or deed, as the case may be. For, although as shewn in the note to p. 1, *ante,* the validity of the discharge may not be susceptible of conclusive proof until after the two months allowed for filing claims have expired ; there appears to be no reason why the proceedings of the insolvent preparatory to applying for confirmation of his discharge should not be going on ; as before he can actually make his application, all parties will be in a position to judge of the sufficiency in number and value of the creditors who have signed, and to contest it if they think proper.
5*

2. *Evil practice—*
Such, for instance, as giving a valuable consideration to procure a consent, or the execution of a deed.   See *post*, p. 13.
3. *Subsequent to the passing of this Act—*
In respect of the punishment of a debtor for not having kept proper books of account, the Act is not retroactive, nor should it be.   But while it does not exact much in the future, the penalty for not doing the little which is necessary in the way of bookkeeping is severe.   A cash book is treated as being essential to every business, but as to his other books the insolvent is permitted to follow the custom of those who cary on the same trade as himself.   If he neglects to keep a book shewing his receipts and disbursements of cash, or neglects to keep such other books as are suitable to his trade, the confirmation of his discharge may be prevented.
4. *If having at any time kept such books he has refused—*
This applies equally to books kept before and to those kept after the passing of the Act.

If confirmation be not demanded within two months proceedings may be taken to annul the discharge.

7. If the insolvent does not apply to the Court or Judge for a confirmation of such discharge within two months from the time at which the same has been effected under this Act, any creditor for a sum exceeding two hundred dollars, may cause to be served a notice in writing upon the insolvent requiring him to file in the Court the consent, or the deed of composition and discharge, as the case may be ; and may thereupon give notice (Form P.) as hereinbefore provided with regard to applications for confirmation of discharge, of his intention to apply by petition to the Court in Lower Canada, or in Upper Canada to the Judge, on a day named in such notice, for

Petition for annulling and proceedings consequent thereon.

the annulling of the discharge ; and on the day so named may present a petition to the Court or Judge, in accordance with such notice, setting forth the reasons in support of such application, which may be any of the reasons upon which a confirmation of discharge may be opposed ; and upon such application, if the insolvent has not, at least one month before the day fixed for the presentation thereof, filed in the office of the Court the consent or deed under which the discharge is effected, the discharge may be annulled without further enquiry, except as to the service upon him of the notice to file the same ; but if such consent or deed be so filed, or if upon special application, leave be granted to him to file the same at a subsequent time, and he do then file the same, the Court or Judge, as the case may be, shall proceed thereon as upon application for confirmation of such discharge ;

Does not apply within two months—
The insolvent would probably be held to have applied within the meaning of this section, if he has deposited the consent or deed of composition, and inserted the required notices.   For the period of two months from the time at which his discharge has been effected, would not enable him actually to present his application to the Court.
This clause merely reverses the order of procedure permitted by the preceding section.   If the debtor omits to bring the validity of his discharge to the test of judicial scrutiny, he may be forced to do so by any creditor who might have opposed its confirmation, had he applied for it.   Neither the proceedings nor the result will be affected by the nature of the issue when once it has been completed ; whether it be joined on the contestation by the creditor of an application for confirmation, or by the insolvent of an application to annul.

8. The Court or Judge, as the case may be, upon hearing Power of Court or Judge. the application to confirm or to annul the discharge, the objections thereto, and any evidence adduced, shall have power to make an order, either confirming the discharge absolutely, suspensively, or conditionally, or annulling the same ; and such order shall be final, unless appealed from in the manner herein provided for as to appeals from the Court or Judge ;

Suspensively or conditionally :—
That is, it may be confirmed ; but its operation may be suspended for such period of time as the Court or Judge may order, as a punishment for any delinquency or impropriety of conduct by the insolvent which is considered reprehensible, but not so much so as to justify the annulling of his discharge. Or it may be confirmed, on condition of the performance by the Insolvent of some act or acts which it is considered his duty to do, but the neglect of which does not involve any fraud, and does not appear to the tribunal of sufficient importance to justify the refusal to confirm his discharge, provided he finally performs it.
These powers may be most beneficially exercised as a check upon the conduct of debtors, by punishing their minor delinquencies, and by compelling their attention to the reasonable requirements of their creditors.

9. Until the Court or Judge, as the case may be, has con- Effect of confirmation. firmed such discharge, the burden of proof of the discharge being completely effected under the provisions of this Act, shall be upon the insolvent ; but the confirmation thereof, if not reversed in appeal, shall render the discharge thereby confirmed, final and conclusive ; and an authentic copy of the judgment confirming the same shall be sufficient evidence, as well of such discharge as of the confirmation thereof ;

Being completely effected—
That is to say, the Insolvent who pleads a discharge which has not been confirmed, must prove that he has obtained the consent of the requisite proportion of his creditors, in number and value ; which, of course, involves establishing the entire amount—and, to some extent, the nature also—of his liabilities ; together with the adduction of such evidence as to the execution of the consent to his discharge, or of the deed of composition and discharge, as the case may be, as is required to prove such execution by the ordinary rules of evidence, at the place where the question is raised.
If the discharge has been confirmed, the mere production of a copy of the judgment confirming it, proves not only such confirmation, but that the discharge itself was "completely effected under the provisions of this Act."

10. If, after the expiration of one year from the date of an When insolvent may apply to the Court or judge for discharge. assignment made under this Act, or from the date of the issue of a writ of attachment thereunder, as the case may be, the insolvent has not obtained, from the required proportion of creditors, a consent to his discharge, or the execution of a deed of composition and discharge, he may apply to the Court in Lower Canada, or to the Judge in Upper Canada by petition, to grant him his discharge, first giving notice of such application, (Form Q.) in the manner hereinbefore provided for notice of application for confirmation of discharge ;

First giving notice :—
Ante p. 6.
The English act allows of such an application 'only after the expiration of
three years from the refusal of a certificate of conformity.

Opposing such
application.

11. Upon such application any creditor of the insolvent may
appear and oppose the granting of such discharge upon any
ground upon which the confirmation of a discharge may be
opposed under this Act ;

Judgment of
Court.

12. The Court or Judge, as the case may be, after hearing
the insolvent, and the objecting creditors, and any evidence
that may be adduced, may make an order either granting the
discharge of the insolvent absolutely, conditionally, or suspensively, or refusing it absolutely ; and such order shall be final,
unless appealed from in the manner herein provided for appeals
from the Court or Judge ;

May make an order :—
The order which the Court or Judge may grant, upon the application of an
Insolvent for a discharge, is substantially the same as that which may be
delivered upon an application for the confirmation of a discharge ; and upon
obtaining such discharge the debtor is in the same position as if he had procured it in the ordinary way and it had been regularly confirmed. See *ante,*
p. 8. And, of course, no proof would be required to support a plea based upon
such discharge, except an authentic copy of the judgment granting it.
The grounds upon which the Court or Judge may refuse a discharge
are not stated in this section, and the sufficiency of the reasons urged by any
creditor against it will therefore be, to some extent, within his discretion.
But the grounds which are declared by the Act to be sufficient, when urged
against the confirmation of a discharge, would probably be regarded in the
same light, if set up against the granting of an order of discharge under
this section.

Discharge, &c.
obtained by
fraud to be
void.

13. Every discharge or composition or confirmation of any
discharge or composition, which has been obtained by fraud or
fraudulent preference, or by means of the consent of any creditor procured by the payment of such creditor of any valuable
consideration for such consent, shall be null and void.

See *ante* p. 6.

EXAMINATION OF THE INSOLVENT AND OTHERS.

When and
how insolvent
may be ex-
amined before
the assignee.

10. Immediately upon the expiry of the period of two months
from the first insertion of the advertisement giving notice of an
assignment, or of the appointment of an official assignee, the
assignee shall call a meeting, by advertisement, of the creditors,
for the public examination of the insolvent, and shall summon
him to attend such meeting ; and at such meeting the insolvent
may be examined on oath, sworn before the assignee, by or on

Examination
to be reduced
to writing.

behalf of any creditor present, in his turn ; and the examination
of the insolvent shall be reduced to writing by the assignee,
and signed by the insolvent; and any questions put to the insolvent at such meeting which he shall answer evasively, or·

refuse to answer, shall also be written in such examination, with the replies made by the insolvent to such questions; and the insolvent shall sign such examination, or if he refuse to sign the same, his refusal shall be entered at the foot of the examination, with the reasons of such refusal, if any, as given by himself; and such examination shall be attested by the assignee and shall be filed in the office of the court; *Signing and attesting it.*

For the public examination of the Insolvent :—
It is not necessary that the meeting at which the public examination of the Insolvent is to take place, should be called for that purpose exclusively; but such examination may be one of the numerous matters which the statute permits to be disposed of at the first general meeting of creditors which is held after the expiry of two months from the date of notice of the appointment of an assignee. § 11, p. 3.

2. *Answer evasively :—*
This is a ground for refusing to confirm a discharge. *ante* p. 6.

3. *Refuse to answer :—*
This kind of conduct on the part of the Insolvent, though not expressly declared to constitute a ground for refusing to confirm his discharge, would, if the questions were reasonable and related to his estate and effects, be a circumstance tending to raise a suspicion of fraudulent concealment or retention of his effects. But, of course, the nature of the presumption that would be raised by such refusal, would depend upon the questions to which it applied. An unreasonable refusal to answer, or to sign his examination, or, in fact, any other contumacy on the part of the Insolvent, should form a sufficient ground, however, for suspending his discharge. But under p. 6, *post*, he could be punished as any other witness might be who conducted himself in a similar manner; and under the same p. he might receive payment for his attendance, like any other witness.

2. The insolvent may also be from time to time examined as to his estate and effects upon oath, before the Judge, by the assignee or by any creditor, upon an order from the Judge obtained without notice to the Insolvent, upon petition, setting forth satisfactory reasons for such order—and he may also be examined in like manner upon a *subpœna* issued as of course without such order, in any action in which a writ of attachment has been issued against his estate and effects; which *subpœna* may be procured by the plaintiff, or by any creditor intervening in the action for that purpose, or by the assignee; *Examination of insolvent before the Judge.*

1. *From time to time examined :—*
This provision enables the assignee to obtain from the debtor any information required, before the time arrives at which his public examination takes place.

2. *Without notice :—* The insolvent has no interest to require a notice, not having any right to oppose his own examination.

3. *Upon a Subpœna :—*
The power of issuing an ordinary *subpœna*, to compel the attendance of the insolvent, in all cases which have been commenced by attachment, renders it unnecessary to obtain the order of a Judge for that purpose, except where proceedings in Insolvency have been commenced by voluntary assignment. And it is a most important privilege, as it may be used by the assignee, if necessary, immediately after his appointment, and afterwards whenever he wishes to procure information respecting the Insolvent's estate and effects.

Examination by assignee or creditor, on application for discharge, &c.

3. The insolvent may also be so examined by the assignee or by any creditor, on the application of the insolvent for a discharge or for the confirmation or annulling of a discharge, at any stage of such proceeding or upon any petition to set aside an attachment in the proceedings for the compulsory liquidation of his estate ;

Other persons may be examined.

4. Any other person who is believed to possess information respecting the estate or effects of the insolvent, may also be from time to time examined before the Judge upon oath, as to such estate or effects, upon an order from the Judge to that effect, which order the Judge may grant upon petition, setting forth satisfactory reasons for such order, without notice to the insolvent or to the person to be so examined ;

Insolvent to attend meetings of his creditors.

5. The insolvent shall attend all meetings of his creditors, when summoned so to do by the assignee, and shall answer all questions that may be put to him at such meetings touching his business, and touching his estate and effects ; and for every such attendance he shall be paid such sum as shall be ordered at such meeting, but not less than one dollar ;

The Insolvent shall attend—
This is a duty imposed upon the insolvent, for the non-performance of which no punishment is prescribed ; but, doubtless, a refusal by the debtor to attend a meeting of his creditors, or, when present, to answer any proper question that is put to him at such a meeting, would be considered, if application were made for the suspension of his discharge.

Conduct of witnesses.

Their costs.

6. Any person summoned for examination or under examination under this Act shall be subject to proceedings and punishments similar to those which may be taken against or inflicted upon ordinary witnesses ; and on application, the Judge may at his discretion order an allowance to be made to persons so examined, of a like amount to that allowed to witnesses in civil cases, and order them to be paid such allowance out of the estate or otherwise.

OF PROCEDURE GENERALLY.

Notices under this Act, how to be given.

11. Notice of meetings of creditors and all other notices herein required to be given by advertisement, without special designation of the nature of such notice, shall be so given by publication thereof for two weeks in the *Canada Gazette*, also in Lower Canada in every issue during two weeks of one newspaper in English and one in French, and in Upper Canada, in one newspaper in English, published at or nearest to the place where the proceedings are being carried on, if such newspapers are published within ten miles of such place ; and in any case the assignee or person giving such notice shall also address notices thereof to all creditors and to all representatives of foreign creditors, within the Province, and shall mail

the same with the postage thereon paid, at the time of the insertion of the first advertisement :

2. All questions discussed at meetings of creditors shall be decided by the majority in number of all creditors for sums above one hundred dollars, present or represented at such meeting, and representing also the majority in value of such creditors, unless herein otherwise specially provided ; but if the majority in number do not agree with the majority in value, the meeting may be adjourned for a period of not less than fifteen days, of which adjournment notice by advertisement shall be given ; and if the adjourned meeting has the same result, the views of each section of the creditors shall be embodied in resolutions, and such resolutions shall be referred to the Judge, who shall decide between them ; *Decision of questions at meetings of creditors.*

3. If the first meeting of creditors which takes place after the expiry of the period of two months from the date of the deed of assignment or of the appointment of an official assignee, be called for the ordering of the affairs of the estate generally, and it be so stated in the notices calling such meeting, all the matters and things respecting which the creditors may vote, resolve or order, or which they may regulate under this Act, may be voted, resolved or ordered upon and may be regulated at such meeting, without having been specially mentioned in the notices calling such meeting, notwithstanding anything to the contrary in this Act contained, due regard being had, however, to the proportions of creditors required by this Act for any such vote, resolution, order or regulation ; · · *What may be done at first meeting of creditors if called for ordering affairs generally, &c.*

Called for the ordering of the affairs of the estate generally—
As has been already remarked, it is of the utmost importance that as many as possible of the matters and things, the direction of which falls within the jurisdiction of the creditors, should be disposed of at this meeting, under the general form of notice provided for by this clause. Among such matters are the following :

1. The enactment of rules, orders and directions for the guidance of the assignee.   § 4, p. 4.

2. The regulation of the security to be given by the assignee.   § 4. p. 6.

3. The reception of the report of the assignee upon the debts remaining uncollected—and the making of the requisite order sanctioning their sale, if thought expedient.   § 4, p. 11.

4. The regulation of the period of advertisement, and of the terms of the sale of the real estate : and of the sale thereof subsequent to a withdrawal of it from public sale—if such withdrawal should be found necessary.   § 4, p. 14.

5. The removal of the assignee, and the appointment of another in his place.   § 4, p. 18.

6. The rate of remuneration of the assignee.   § 4, p. 20.

7. Whether or no collateral security valued by a claimant, shall be assumed by the estate or not.   § 5, p. 5.

8. The granting of an allowance to the insolvent.   § 5, p. 8.

9. Whether or not the costs of any specified contestation shall be paid out of the estate.   § 5, p. 15.

10. The continuance or cessation of the lease of the premises occupied by the Insolvent.   § 6, p. 2.

11. The public examination of the insolvent.   § 10, p. 1.

Claims of creditors; form of. 4. The claims of creditors (Form R) shall be furnished to the assignee in writing, and shall specify what security, if any, the creditor holds for the payment of his claim, and when required by this Act shall also contain an estimate by such creditor of the value of such security ; and if the creditor holds no security, then it shall also be so therein stated ;

1. *In writing—*
As to the mode of filing claims, their headings, endorsement and subscription, see Rule 6.
2. *Value required by this Act—*
See § 5, p. 5.
3. *An estimate—*
Upon this estimate being made, the future proceedings with regard to the security are decided upon. If the estimate is considered reasonable, the creditor is allowed to retain the security, and the value he fixes upon it is deducted from his claim. If the estimate is not considered sufficient, the assignee may assume the security for the benefit of the estate at ten per centum advance upon the estimate, and the creditor ranks for the difference. § 5, p. 5.

How to be attested. 5. The claims shall be attested under oath, taken in Canada before any Judge, Commissioner for taking Affidavits, or Justice of the Peace, and out of Canada, before any Judge of a Court of Record, any Commissioner for taking Affidavits appointed by any Canadian Court, the Chief Municipal Officer for any Town or City, or any British Consul or Vice-Consul, or before any other person authorized by any statute of this Province for taking affidavits to be used in this Province ;

Supplementary oath in certain cases. 6. Before the preparation of a dividend sheet, the assignee may require from any creditor a supplementary oath declaring what amount, if any, such creditor has received in part payment of the debt upon which his claim is founded, subsequent to the making of such claim, together with the particulars of such payment ; and if any creditor refuses to produce or make such oath before the assignee within a reasonable time after he has been required so to do, he shall not be collocated in such dividend sheet ;

Such creditor has received in part payment.—
The object of this clause is to afford the means of carrying out the provisions of § 5, p. 6. If the claim of a creditor is composed of several items— say for instance, of several promissory notes or bills bearing different names, upon some of which the insolvent is only secondarily liable, and the maker, acceptor or a previous endorser should pay one of such notes or bills in full ;—the amount of such note or bill should be deducted from the claim, and all ranking upon it should cease. And by the supplementary oath, which may be required from the claimant under this clause, the assignee can ascertain whether or no any such payment has been made.
It is only in such a case as the foregoing that the oath is of use—as no ordinary payment on account, will give the assignee the right of demanding a deduction from the amount ranked for. See note to § 5, p. 6, and authorities there cited.

7. If, in Lower Canada, any claim be secured by *hypothèque* upon the real estate of the insolvent, or if it consists of any *hypothèque* or *privilege* upon such real estate or any part thereof, the nature of such *hypothèque* or *privilege* shall be summarily specified in such claim ; but unless such claim be filed with the assignee, with the deeds and documents in support thereof, within six days from the day of sale of the property affected thereby, or if not, unless leave to file the same be afterwards obtained from the Judge upon special cause shewn, previous to the distribution of the proceeds of such real estate, or unless a dividend upon such claim has been reserved by the assignee, such claim shall not be entitled to any preferential collocation upon the proceeds of such real estate ;

Claims secured by hypothèque or privilège in L. C.

Documents to be filed, &c.

Unless a dividend * * * *has been reserved.* —
If no claim be filed for any debt which the assignee has reason to believe is due—it is his duty to reserve a dividend upon the amount of such debt. § 5, p. 12.

8. Any affidavit required under this Act may be made by the party interested, or by the agent in that behalf having a personal knowledge of the matters therein stated ;

Who may make affidavits under this Act.

9. One clear day's notice of any petition, motion or rule, shall be sufficient if the party notified resides within fifteen miles of the place where the proceeding is to be taken, and one extra day shall be sufficient allowance for each additional fifteen miles of distance between the place of service and the place of proceeding, and service of such notice shall be made in such manner as is now prescribed for similar services in that section of the Province within which the service is made ;

Notices of proceedings.

Service of such notice. —
Rules 17 and 18 make provisions for such services, in a manner similar to that adopted under the previous practice in like cases in Lower Canada.

10. The Judge shall have the same power and authority in respect of the issuing and dealing with Commissions for the examination of witnesses, as are possessed by the ordinary Courts of Record in the section of the Province in which the proceedings are being carried on ;

Commissions for examination of witnesses.

Commissions. —
See Cons. Stat. L. C. pp. 737-8.

11. All rules, orders and warrants, issued by any Judge or court in any matter or proceeding under this Act, may be validly served in any part of this Province upon the party affected or to be affected thereby ; and the service of them or any of them may be validly made in such manner as is now prescribed for singular services in that part of the Province within which the service is made ; and the person charged with such service shall make his return thereof and on oath, or,

Rules, &c., may be served in any part of this Province.

if a sheriff or bailiff in Lower Canada, may make such return under his oath of office ;

1. *In any part of this Province.*—
That is to say that such documents may be served in a part of the Province different from that in which the Judge or Court issuing them, has jurisdiction. So that a Judge at Montreal may issue a rule, order or warrant which may be validly served in Upper Canada.

2. *Service of them may be validly made.*—
That is to say the service of a rule, order or warrant issued in Lower Canada will be validly made in Upper Canada, if that mode of service be adopted which is usual for similar proceedings in Upper Canada.

Certain ss. of caps. 79 and 80, Con. Stat. of Canada to apply.

12. The fourth, fifth, seventh, eighth, ninth, tenth, eleventh and thirteenth sections of chapter seventy-nine of the Consolidated Statutes of Canada shall apply to proceedings under this Act ; and the whole of chapter eighty of the said Consolidated Statutes shall also apply to proceedings under this Act, in the same manner and to the same extent as to proceedings before Courts of Record in Upper and Lower Canada ;

1. *The 4th, 5th, * * * * sections of Cap. 79.*
These sections provide for the issue of subpœnas running from one section of the Province into the other ; for the service of such subpœnas, and its proof ; for the punishment of the parties summoned if they do not attend, and the allowances to be made to them if they do.

2. *Chapter Eighty.*—
This chapter facilitates the admission as evidence in Upper Canada of judgments, decrees and judicial proceedings rendered or made in Great Britain, the United States, or Lower Canada.—And also simplifies the mode of proof of official acts, judgments, and judicial proceedings generally. There is a similar and more complete statute in Lower Canada, forming Chapter 90, of the Consolidated Statutes for that section—which will apply under its own provisions, to proceedings under this Act.

Forms appended to be used.
In other cases ordinary language to be sufficient.

13. The forms appended to this Act, or other forms in equivalent terms, shall be used in the proceedings for which such forms are provided ; but in every petition, application, motion, contestation, or other pleading under this Act, the parties may state the facts upon which they rely in plain and concise language, to the interpretation of which the rules of construction applicable to such language in the ordinary transactions of life shall apply ; and no allegation or statement shall be held to be insufficiently made, unless by reason of any alleged insufficiency the opposing party be misled or taken by surprise ;

Amendment of proceedings.

14. The rules of procedure as to amendments of pleadings, which are in force at any place where any proceedings under this Act are carried on, shall apply to all proceedings under this Act ; and any judge before whom any such proceedings are being carried on shall have full power and authority to apply the appropriate rules as to amendments, to the proceedings so pending before him ; and no pleading or proceeding shall be void by reason of any irregularity or default which can or may be amended under the rules and practice of the court ;

15. The death of the insolvent, pending proceedings upon a Effect of death of insolvent pending proceedings. voluntary assignment or in compulsory liquidation, shall not affect such proceedings, or impede the winding up of his estate ; and his heirs or other legal representatives may continue the proceedings on his behalf to the procuring of a discharge, or of the confirmation thereof, or of both ;

16. The costs of the action to compel compulsory liquidation Costs to compel compulsory liquidation. shall be paid by privilege as a first charge upon the assets of the insolvent; and the costs of the judgment of confirmation of the discharge of the insolvent, or of the discharge if obtained direct from the Court, and the costs of winding up the estate, being first submitted at a meeting of creditors, and afterwards taxed by the judge, shall also be paid therefrom ;

17. In Lower Canada rules of practice for regulating the due Rules of practice and tariff of fees in L. C. conduct of proceedings under this Act before the Court or Judge, and tariffs of fees for the Officers of the Court, and for the Advocates and Attorneys practising in relation to such proceedings, shall be made forthwith after the passing of this Act, and when necessary repealed or amended, and shall be promulgated, under or by the same authority and in the same manner as the rules of practice and tariff of fees of the Superior Court for Lower Canada, and shall apply in the same manner and have the same effect in respect of the proceedings under Taxation of costs. this Act, as the rules of practice and tariff of fees of the Superior Court apply to and affect the proceedings before that Court ; and bills of costs upon proceedings under this Act, may be taxed and proceeded upon in like manner, as bills of costs may now be taxed and proceeded upon in the said Superior Court ;

18. In Upper Canada the Judges of the Superior Courts of Rules and tariff in U. C. Common Law, and of the Court of Chancery, or any five of them, of whom the Chief Justice of Upper Canada, or the Chancellor, or the Chief Justice of the Common Pleas, shall be one, shall have power to frame and settle such forms, rules and regulations as shall be followed and observed in the proceedings on insolvency under this Act, as they may deem to be necessary, and to fix and settle the costs, fees and charges which shall or may be had, taken or paid in all such cases by or to Attorneys, Solicitors, Counsel, Officers of Courts, whether for the Officer or for the Crown, as a fee for the fee fund or otherwise, Sheriffs, Assignees or other persons whom it may be necessary to provide for.

GENERAL PROVISIONS.

12. In all cases of sales of merchandise to a trader in Rights of unpaid vendor under Cou- Lower Canada subsequently becoming insolvent, the exercise of the rights and privileges conferred upon the unpaid vendor by

tume de Paris, the one hundred and seventy-sixth and one hundred and
restricted. seventy-seventh articles of the *Coutume de Paris*, is hereby
restricted to a period of fifteen days from the delivery of such
merchandise :

The rights and privileges of the unpaid vendor.—
The right of revendicating goods sold *à terme* has been pressed very far
in Lower Canada, and has frequently resulted in great injustice to the
general creditors of an insolvent estate. It appears to have been considered
that the duration of the period between the sale and the revendication was
of no consequence ; nor were the effects relieved from the operation of the
law, by the fact of the purchaser having given promissory notes for such
purchase, nor in consequence of such notes having passed out of his possession by being discounted. Consequently a debtor with a large stock
of goods on hand ; and therefore with, and on the strength of, an apparent abundance of assets ; might obtain long credit on the purchase of the
most saleable goods in the market. He might sell the whole of such goods,
expend the money and fail ; and every dollar's worth of the very goods
which gave him the appearance of solvency might be appropriated by
their vendors ; leaving nothing for the other creditors, although their
claims might be for sales made subsequently to those which were thus
virtually paid in full.
It is plain that the existence of the right of thus revendicating goods sold—
though alleged to be an encouragement of trade and an aid to credit—was,
in reality, the reverse ; for it deprived of all weight the presumption of pros-
perity which would otherwise naturally have arisen from the possession of
an ample stock of goods.
This evil was felt strongly in France ; and in the discussion of the *code de
commerce* and of the amendments of 1838, the great majority of the cham-
bers of commerce expressed themselves forcibly, against the right of revendication allowed by the common law. By the law, as it now stands, the
right of revendication has a character almost identical with that of the English stoppage *in transitu.* In order that goods sold may be revendicated
they should be delivered ; that is, they should have passed out of the actual
possession of the vendor ; they should not be paid for—and they should not
have entered the warehouses of the purchaser. Art. 576. 3. Bed. p. 193.
And the latter condition is not construed over strictly, if, by doing so, room is
given for the occurrence of the great abuse to which this right gave rise.
M. Bedarride says : "*La revendication a été surtout admise parce que la
marchandise n'a encore aux yeux de personne, augmenté le crédit et l'actif
de celui qui est devenu propriétaire sans en être possesseur.*" And he argues
from this that if the goods have passed into the actual possession of the vendor, so that they may have, in some one's eyes, *augmenté le crédit et
l'actif* of the debtor, the right of revendication will be lost, though the goods
may not have actually passed into his warehouse. 3 Bed. p. 199.
Acting upon similar opinions as to the impropriety of permitting to the
right of revendication too extensive a character, the Legislature has materi-
ally restricted its exercise, by limiting it—in the case of sales of merchandise to a trader—to the period of fifteen days from the date of the delivery of
the goods

In L. C. mar-
riage con-
tracts of
traders to be
registered
within a cer-
tain period.

2. In Lower Canada, every trader who marries, having previously executed a contract of marriage by which he gives or
promises to give or to pay, or cause to be paid to his wife, any
property or effects, or any sum of money, shall cause such
contract of marriage to be enregistered in the registration
division in which he has his place of business, within thirty
days from the execution thereof ; and every trader already
married, having such marriage contract with his wife, shall

enregister the same as aforesaid, if it be not there already enregistered, within three months from the passing of this Act; and every person not a trader, but hereafter becoming a trader, and having such a contract of marriage with his wife, shall cause such contract to be enregistered as aforesaid (if it be not previously there enregistered), within thirty days from becoming such trader; and in default of such registration the wife shall not be permitted to avail herself of its provisions in any claim upon the estate of such insolvent for any advantage conferred upon or promised to her by its terms; nor shall she be deprived by reason of its provisions of any advantage or right upon the estate of her husband, to which, in the absence of any such contract, she would have been entitled by law;

Provision in default of such registration.

In any claim upon the estate—
This clause, however, would not prevent the wife from holding property, if she be *séparée de biens* by her marriage contract. The contract is only rendered useless to her to support any claim upon her husband's estate.

2. *Nor shall she be deprived * * * * of any advantage—*
If, for instance, she has, by her marriage contract, renounced her customary dower and received the promise of a sum of money, or of the usufruct of a sum of money, in lieu of such dower,—she will be unable to claim the money or usufruct so settled upon her, but she may insist upon her dower under the custom.

The reason is, that if no contract be registered, the creditors are entitled to presume that none has been executed. But, if that presumption be acted upon, the whole of its consequences must follow, and, amongst others, the existence of *douaire coutumier*, which, in the absence of a contract, would undoubtedly belong to her.

3. No judgment shall be rendered against any trader in Lower Canada in any action against him by his wife *en sépa-ration de biens* or *en séparation de corps et de biens*, unless the institution of such action is advertised continuously for one month in the *Canada Gazette*, and in two newspapers published in or nearest to the place of residence of such trader, one in French, the other in English; nor unless such action be brought in the district within which the defendant has his domicile; and any creditor of the defendant in any such suit may inter-vene therein for the purpose of examining such debtor respect-ing his estate and effects, without becoming liable for any costs either to the plaintiff or to the defendant, and may also intervene therein, and oppose the demand of the plaintiff, or subsequently contest the validity of any judgment rendered therein, subject to the ordinary rule as to costs;

Judgments in actions en sé-paration de biens, to be rendered only on certain conditions.

Creditors may intervene.

The experience of the last few years in Lower Canada renders unneces-sary any explanation of the purposes of this clause. Those merchants will understand them, from whom goods have been purchased by a trader while his wife's suit *en séparation de biens* has been actually proceeding to judg-ment *ex parte*, who, after getting judgment for the price of them, have found his wife in possession of their own goods, amidst a shop-full of others so pur-chased—acquired by her, under execution, for what will pay her lawyer for obtaining her judgment *en séparation ;* and who have beheld the husband carrying on a prosperous business—as his wife's agent—with their capital, and laughing to scorn their attempts to recover even the additional hundred dollars they have lost in endeavoring to enforce payment. And it is probable that there are few (if any) wholesale merchants in Lower Canada who have not possessed at least one opportunity of thus appreciating the advantages of a judgment *en séparation de biens*, and of paying liberally for the privilege.

Interpretation.

"Before Notaries."
"Judge."
"Court."

Certain provisions to apply.

4. The words "before Notaries" shall mean executed in Notarial form according to the law of Lower Canada ; the words "the Judge" shall, in Lower Canada, signify a Judge of the Superior Court for Lower Canada, having jurisdiction at the domicile of the insolvent ; and in Upper Canada a Judge of the County Court of the County or Union of Counties in which the proceedings are carried on, and the words. "the Court" shall, in Lower Canada, signify the said Superior Court, and in Upper Canada the County Court, unless it is otherwise expressed or unless the context plainly requires a different construction ; but the twenty-fourth and twenty-fifth sections of the seventy-eighth chapter of the Consolidated Statutes for Lower Canada, including subsection number two of the said twenty-fifth section, shall apply in Lower Canada to proceedings under this Act ;

The 24th and 25th sections of the seventy-eighth chapter—
These sections permit of the action of the Prothonotary of the Superior Court in lieu of the Judge, in certain cases, and provide a summary mode of revising the acts of the Prothonotary under the powers thus conferred upon him.

"Assignee."

"Day."
"Creditor."

"Collocated."

Application of Act to companies, &c.

5. The word "Assignee" shall mean the official assignee appointed in proceedings for compulsory liquidation as well as the assignee appointed under a deed of voluntary assignment ; the word "day" shall mean a juridical day ; the word "Creditor" shall be held to mean every person to whom the insolvent is liable, whether primarily or secondarily, and whether as principal or surety ; but no debt shall be doubly represented or ranked for, either in the computation for ascertaining the numbers and proportion of creditors, or in the allotment or payment of dividends ; the word "collocated" shall mean ranked or placed in the dividend sheet for some dividend or sum of money ; and all the provisions of this Act respecting traders, shall be held to apply equally to unincorporated trading Companies and co-partnerships ; and the chief office or place of business of such unincorporated trading Companies and co-partnerships shall be their domicile for the purposes of this Act ;

No debt shall be doubly represented or ranked for—
See note to § 5, p. 6.

Assignees to be agents within the meaning of

6. Every assignee to whom an assignment is made under this Act, and every official assignee appointed under the provisions of this Act, is an agent within the meaning of the forty-third, forty-fourth, forty-sixth, forty-eighth and forty-ninth

sections of the ninety-second chapter of the Consolidated Statutes of Canada ; and every provision of this Act, or resolution of the creditors, relating to the duties of an assignee or official assignee, shall be held to be direction in writing, within the meaning of the said forty-third section of the said chapter ; and in an indictment against an assignee or official assignee under any of the said sections, the right of property in any moneys, security, matter, or thing, may be laid in " the creditors of the insolvent (*naming him*), under the Insolvent Act of 1864," or in the name of any assignee subsequently appointed, in his quality as such assignee ; *Con. Stat. Canada, cap. 92, sec. 43, &c.*

7. The deed of assignment, or an authentic copy thereof, or a duly authenticated copy of the order of the judge appointing an official assignee, or a duly certified extract from the minutes of a meeting of creditors, according to the mode in which the assignee or official assignee is alleged to be appointed, shall be *primâ facie* evidence in all courts, whether civil or criminal, of such appointment, and of the regularity of all proceedings at the time thereof and antecedent thereto ; *Deed of assignment, &c., to be primâ facie evidence.*

8. One per centum upon all moneys proceeding from the sale by an assignee, under the provisions of this Act, of any immoveable property in Lower Canada, shall be retained by the assignee out of such moneys, and shall by such assignee be paid over to the Sheriff of the District, or of either of the counties of Gaspé or Bonaventure, as the case may be, within which the immoveable property sold shall be situate, to form part of the Building and Jury Fund of such District or County ; *Percentage for Building and Jury Fund in L. C*

9. The Governor in Council shall have all the powers with respect to imposing a tax or duty upon proceedings under this Act, which are conferred upon the Governor in Council by the thirty-second and thirty-third sections of the one hundred and ninth chapter of the Consolidated Statutes for Lower Canada, and by the Act intituled : *An Act to make provision for the erection or repair of Court Houses and Gaols at certain places in Lower Canada*, (12 Vic., cap. 112.) *Power to impose a tax on proceedings in L. C.*

13. This Act shall be called and known as " The Insolvent Act of 1864," and shall come into force and take effect on and after the first day of September next. *Short title.*

FORM A.

INSOLVENT ACT OF 1864.

The Creditors of the undersigned are notified to meet at in   on   the   *th* day of at (*eight*) o'clock   for the purpose of receiving statements of his affairs, and of naming an Assignee to whom he may make an assignment under the above Act.

(*Domicile of debtor, and date.*)

(*Signature.*)

(*The following is to be added to the notices sent by post.*)

The Creditors holding direct claims and indirect claims, maturing before the meeting, for one hundred dollars each and upwards, are as follows : (*names of Creditors and amount due*) and the aggregate of claims under one hundred dollars is $

(*Domicile of debtor, and date.*)

(*Signature.*)

FORM B.

INSOLVENT ACT OF 1864.

In the matter of A. B., an insolvent.

Schedule of Creditors.

1. Direct Liabilities.

Name.	Residence.	Nature of Debt.	Amount.	Total.

2. Indirect liabilities, maturing before the day fixed for the first meeting of creditors.

Name.	Residence.	Nature of Debt.	Amount.

3. Indirect liabilities, maturing after the day fixed for the first meeting of creditors.

Name.	Residence.	Nature of Debt.	Amount.

4. Negotiable paper, the holders of which are unknown.

Date.	Name of Maker.	Names liable to Insolvent.	When due.	Amount.

6 *

Province of Canada, }
District (or *County*) }   INSOLVENT ACT OF 1864.

I, A. B., the above named insolvent, being duly sworn,
depose and say :

1. That to the best of my knowledge and belief, and according to my books, the above schedule contains a true and correct list of my liabilities, according to its purport, and that each
of such liabilities is correctly classified therein.

2. That all of the above-mentioned liabilities are honestly
due by me and that none of them were created or have been
increased with the intention of giving to the creditor thereof
any advantage either in voting at meetings of creditors, or in
ranking on my estate. And I have signed.

Sworn before me at   this   day of
186 .

_____

FORM C.

INSOLVENT ACT OF 1864.

This assignment made between   of the
first part, and   of the second part,
witnesses,

(*or*)

On this   day of
before the undersigned notaries
came and appeared
of the first part, and
of the second part, which said parties declared to us Notaries.

That under the provisions of "the Insolvent Act of 1864"
the said party of the first part, being insolvent, has voluntarily
assigned and hereby does voluntarily assign to the said party
of the second part, accepting thereof as assignee under the said
Act, and for the purposes therein provided, all his estate and
effects real and personal of every nature and kind whatsoever.

To have and to hold to the party of the second part as
assignee for the purposes and under the Act aforesaid.

And a duplicate of the list of creditors exhibited at the first
meeting of his creditors, by the said party of the first part, is
hereto annexed.

In witness whereof, &c.

or

Done and passed, &c.

FORM D.

INSOLVENT ACT OF 1864.

In the matter of

A. B. (*or* **A. B. & Co.)**
an Insolvent.

The creditors of the insolvent are notified that he has made an assignment of his estate and effects, under the above Act, to me, the undersigned assignee, and they are required to furnish me, within two months from this date, with their claims, specifying the security they hold, if any, and the value of it ; and if none, stating the fact ; the whole attested under oath, with the vouchers in support of such claims.

> (*Place   date*)
> (*Signature of assignee.*)

FORM E.

INSOLVENT ACT OF 1864.

To (*name   residence   and description*
of insolvent.)

You are hereby required to make an assignment of your estate and effects under the above Act, for the benefit of your creditors.

> *Place   date*
> (*Signature of creditor.*)   .

FORM F.

INSOLVENT ACT OF 1864.

PROVINCE OF CANADA, }
  DISTRICT OF   }

A. B———, (*name, residence and description.*)
                                        Plaintiff.
                        vs.
C. D———, (*name, residence and description.*)
                                        Defendant.

I, A. B———, (*name, residence and description*) being duly sworn, depose and say :

1. I am the Plaintiff in this cause (*or one of the Plaintiffs, or the clerk, or the agent of the Plaintiff in this cause duly authorized for the purposes hereof ;*

2. The defendant is indebted to the Plaintiff (*or as the case may be*) in the sum of   dollars currency for, (*state concisely and clearly the nature of the debt*) ;

3. To the best of my knowledge and belief the defendant is insolvent within the meaning of the Insolvent Act of 1864, and has rendered himself liable to have his estate placed in compulsory liquidation under the above mentioned Act ; and my reasons for so believing are as follows : (*state concisely the facts relied upon as rendering the debtor insolvent, and as subjecting his estate to be placed in compulsory liquidation.*)

And I have signed ; (*or* I declare that I cannot sign,) this   day of   186 .

and if the deponent cannot sign, add—*the foregoing affidavit having been first read over by me to the deponent.*

(FORM G.)

INSOLVENT ACT OF 1864.

PROVINCE OF CANADA, District of Quebec. VICTORIA, *by the Grace of God, of the United Kingdom of Great Britain and Ireland, Queen, Defender of the Faith.*

To the Sheriff of our District (*or* County) of
No.   GREETING :

WE command you at the instance of
to attach the estate and effects, moneys and securities for money, vouchers, and all the office and business papers and documents of every kind and nature whatsoever
of and belonging to
if the same shall be found in (*name of district or other territorial jurisdiction*) and the same so attached, safely to hold, keep and detain in your charge and custody, until the attachment thereof, which shall be so made under and by virtue of this Writ, shall be determined in due course of Law.

We command you also to summon the said
to be and appear before Us, in our   Court for   at   in the County (or District) of   on the   day of
then and there to answer the said
of the plaint contained in the declaration hereto annexed, and further to do and receive what, in our said Court before Us,

in this behalf shall be considered ;¹ and in what manner you
shall have executed this Writ, then and there certify unto Us
with your doings thereon, and every of them, and have you
then and there also this Writ.

In Witness Whereof, We have caused the Seal of our
said Court to be hereunto affixed, at   aforesaid
            , this   day of
in the year of our Lord, one thousand eight hundred and
sixty-   in the

(FORM H.)

INSOLVENT ACT OF 1864.

A. B.,
        Plff.
C. D.,
        Deft.

A writ of attachement has issued in this cause, of which
all persons interested in the estate of the defendant, and all
persons having in their possession, custody or power, any
portion of the assets of the defendant, or who are in any way
indebted to him, are required to take notice.

(*Place*   *date.*   )
            (*Signature,*)
                            Sheriff.

(FORM I.)

INSOLVENT ACT OF 1864.

I swear that I (*or, the firm of which I am a member, or, A.
B. of   of whom I am the duly authorized agent in
this behalf,*) am (*or* is) a creditor of the Insolvent, and that I
will give my advice in the appointment of an assignee to his
estate, honestly and faithfully and in the interest of his creditors generally.

(FORM K.)

INSOLVENT ACT OF 1864.

In the matter of
            A. B. (*or* A. B. & Co.),
                        an insolvent.

The creditors of the insolvent are notified that I, the undersigned (*name and residence*), have been appointed official

assignee of his estate and effects : and they are required to produce before me within two months from this date, their claims upon the said estate under oath, specifying the security they hold, if any, and the value of it, and if none, stating the fact, with vouchers in support of such claims.

(*Place*   *date,*)
                              (*Signature,*)
                              Official Assignee.

(FORM L.)

Insolvent Act of 1864.

In the matter of

A. B.,
an insolvent.

In consideration of the sum of $ whereof quit ; C. D., assignee of the insolvent, in that capacity hereby sells and assigns to E. F. accepting thereof, all claim by the Insolvent against G. H. of (*describing the debtor*) with the evidences of debt and securities thereto appertaining, but without any warranty of any kind or nature whatsoever.

C. D., *Assignee*
E. F.

FORM M.

This deed, made under the provisions of the Insolvent Act of 1864, the   day of   &c., between A. B. of   &c., in his capacity of assignee of the estate and effects of an insolvent, under a deed of assignment executed on the   day of   at   in Canada, (*or under an order of the Judge made at* *on the   day of*   ) of the one part, and C. D., of   &c., of the other part, witnesseth : That he, the said A. B., in his said capacity, hath caused the sale of the real estate hereinafter mentioned, to be advertised in the *Canada Gazette* from the   day of   to the day of   inclusive, and hath adjudged and doth hereby grant, bargain, sell, and confirm the same, to wit : unto the said C.D., his heirs and assigns for ever, all (*in Upper Canada insert " the rights and interests of the Insolvent in "*) that certain lot of land, &c., (*insert here a description of the property sold*): To have and to hold the same, with the

appurtenances thereof, unto the said C.D., his heirs and assigns for ever. The said sale is so made for and in consideration of the sum of $
in hand paid by the said C.D. to the said A.B., the receipt whereof is hereby acknowledged (*or* of which the said C.D. hath paid to the said A.B. the sum of
the receipt whereof is hereby acknowledged) and the balance, or sum of $ the said C.D. hereby promises to pay the said A.B., in his said capacity, as follows, to wit---(*here state the terms of payment*)---the whole with interest payable   and, as security for the payments so to be made, the said C.D. hereby specially mortgages and hypothecates to and in favour of the said A.B., in his said capacity, the lot of land and premises hereby sold. In witness,

A.B.	[L.S.]
C.D.	[L.S.]

Signed, sealed, and delivered
   in the presence of

    E.F

FORM N.

INSOLVENT ACT OF 1864.

In the matter of

A.B (*or* A.B. & Co.,)
         an Insolvent.

The Creditors of the Insolvent are notified that a dividend sheet has been prepared, and will remain open to inspection and objection at my office (*describing it*) every day between the hours of ten and five o'clock until the
day of   after which the dividends therein allotted will be paid.

FORM O.

INSOLVENT ACT OF 1864.

PROVINCE OF CANADA, } In the (*name of Court*)
District (*or County*) of }   (In the matter of A.B. (*or*
        A.B. & Co.), an Insolvent.

Notice is hereby given that the undersigned has filed in the office of this Court, a consent by his creditors to his discharge (*or a deed of composition and discharge, executed by his*

creditors), and that on   the   day of
          next, at ten of the clock in the forenoon, or as
soon as counsel can be heard, he will apply to the said Court
(*or to the Judge of the said Court, as the case may be*) for a confirmation of the discharge thereby effected in his favor, under
the said Act.

(*Place   date.*)

(Signature of Insolvent, or of his Attorney *ad litem*).

FORM P.

INSOLVENT ACT OF 1864.

PROVINCE OF CANADA, } In the (*name of Court*)
District (*or County*) of }   In the matter of A. B., an
          Insolvent.

Notice is hereby given that the undersigned creditor of the
insolvent has required him to file, in the office of this Court,
the consent of his creditors, or the deed of composition and
discharge executed by them, under which he claims to be
discharged under the said Act ; and that on   the
          day of   next, at ten of the clock in
the forenoon, or as soon as counsel can be heard, the
undersigned will apply to the said Court (*or to the Judge of
the said Court, as the case may be*) for the annulling of such
discharge.

    (*Place   date.*)
  (Signature of Insolvent, or of his Attorney *ad litem.*

FORM Q.

INSOLVENT ACT OF 1864.

PROVINCE OF CANADA, } In the (*name of Court*)
District (*or County*) of }   In the matter of A.B. (or A.B
         & Co.) an Insolvent.

Notice is hereby given that on   the   day of
          next, at ten of the clock in the forenoon, or as soon
as counsel can be heard, the undersigned will apply to the
said Court (*or* the Judge of the said Court, *as the case may
be*) for a discharge under the said Act.

   (*Place,   date.*)
  (Signature of the Insolvent, or his Attorney *ad litem.*)

FORM R.

INSOLVENT ACT OF 1864.

In the matter of
A. B.,
    An Insolvent, and
C. D.,
    Claimant.

I, C. D., of   , being duly sworn in
depose and say:

1. I am the claimant (or, *the duly authorized agent of the claimant in this behalf, and have a personal knowledge of the matter hereinafter deposed to, or a member of the firm of claimants in the matter, and the said firm is composed of myself and of E. F. of*)

2. The insolvent is indebted to me (or *to the claimant*) in the sum of   dollars, for (*here state the nature and particulars of the claim, for which purpose reference may also be made to accounts or documents annexed.*)

3. I (or *the claimant*) hold no security for the claim, (or *I or the claimant holds the following, and no other, security for the claim, namely: (state the particulars of the security.)*

To the best of my knowledge and belief, the security is of the value of   dollars.

Sworn before me at
this   day of   } And I have signed.

RULES AND ORDERS

TARIFF OF FEES,

Made by the Judges of the Superior Court for Lower Canada, under
and by virtue of the Statute 27 and 28 Vict., cap. 17,
intituled : " An Act respecting Insolvency."

1. There shall be assigned in the Court House of each Judicial
District at which the sittings of the Superior Court are held, two
rooms for matters in Insolvency, one in which the sittings of the
Judge shall be held, and the other for the Office of the Clerk
in Insolvency.

2. All judicial proceedings in Insolvency shall be had and
conducted in the said Court Room alone, and not elsewhere ; and
the sittings of the Judge shall commence at 11 A. M., or at such
hour as the Judges or Judge in each District shall hereafter
appoint, and shall continue till the business of the day shall be
completed, or until the Judge shall adjourn the same.

3. The Clerk's Office shall be kept open every juridical day, from
9 A. M. to 4 P. M., and shall be attended during that time by a
Clerk appointed by the District Prothonotary, and who shall be
known as " The Clerk in Insolvency."

4. To ensure regularity of proceedings at the sittings of the
Judges, the business shall be conducted in the following order :

      1. Meetings of Creditors ;
      2. Motions ;
      3. Rules Nisi ;
      4. Petitions, except as hereinafter mentioned ;
      5. Proceedings on applications for discharge of Insolvents ;
      6. Proceedings on applications for discharge of Assignee ;
      7. Appeals.

5. Proceedings before a Judge or Court may be conducted by
the Insolvent himself, or by any party having interest therein, or
by their Attorney *ad litem*, admitted to practice in Lower Canada,
and by no other person.

6. All Motions, Petitions and Claims, and all papers in the nature of pleadings in Insolvency shall be intituled : In Insolvency, for the District of .... In the matter of .... Insolvent, and .... Claimant, Petitioner or Applicant, as the case may be, plainly written, without interlineations or abbreviations of words ; and the subject or purpose thereof shall be plainly and concisely stated. They shall also be subscribed by the Petitioner, Applicant or Claimant, or by his Attorney *ad litem* for him. And they shall be subject to the ordinary rules of procedure of the Superior Court in respect of similar papers, as regards the names and designations of the parties, and the mode in which they shall be docketed and filed.

7. No paper of any description shall be received or filed in any case, unless the same shall be properly numbered and intituled in the case or proceeding to which it may refer or belong ; and be also endorsed with the general description thereof, and with the name of the party or his Attorney *ad litem* filing the same.

8. In all appealable matter in dispute, the pretensions of the parties shall be set forth in writing, in a clear, precise and intelligible manner, and the notes of the verbal evidence taken before the Assignee shall be plainly written, shall be signed by the witness, if he can write and sign his name, and shall be certified by the Assignee as having been sworn before him. And in the event of an appeal, the Assignee shall make and certify a transcript from his Register, of the proceedings before him in the matter appealed from. And he shall also make and certify a list of the documents composing such proceedings and appertaining thereto, and shall annex such transcript and list to such documents with a strong paper or parchment cover, before producing the record before the Judge, as required by the said Act.

9. All proceedings before a Judge or Court shall be entered daily, in order of date, in a docket of proceedings, to be kept by the Clerk for each case ; and shall, from time to time, and until the close of the Estate, be fairly transcribed in Registers suitable therefor, which shall be kept and preserved by the Prothonotary, in the same manner as the Registers of proceedings of the Superior Court.

10. No Demand, Petition or Application of which notice is required to be given, either by the provisions of the said Act or by an order of the Judge or Court, shall be heard until after such notice shall have been given, and due return thereof made and filed in the case.

11. Except where otherwise limited and provided by the said Act, and upon good cause shewn, the time for proceeding after notice thereof has been given, may be enlarged by the Judge or Court whenever the rights of parties interested may seem to require it for the purposes of justice.

12. Whenever a particular number of days is prescribed for the doing of an Act in Insolvency, the first and last day shall not be

computed, nor any fractions of a day allowed ; and when the last day shall fall upon a Sunday or Holiday, the time shall be enlarged to the next juridical day.

13. All affidavits of indebtedness made by a creditor, or by the clerk or agent of a creditor, shall set forth the particulars and nature of the debt, with the same degree of certainty and precision as is required in affidavits to hold to bail in civil process in the Courts of Lower Canada.

14. All Writs of Attachment issued under the said Act, shall, as issued, be numbered and entered successively by the Clerk in a Book, to which there shall be an Index, and to which access for examination or extract shall be had *gratis*, at all times during office hours.

15. Every such Writ shall describe the parties thereto, in the same manner as they are described in the said affidavits of debt ; and the Declaration accompanying the said Writ, shall be similar in its form to the Declarations required to be filed in ordinary suits in the Superior Court.

16. No such Writ shall issue until after the affidavit of debt upon which the Writ is founded, shall have been duly filed in the Clerk's Office.

17. All services of Writs, Rules, Notices, Warrants and proceedings in Lower Canada, except otherwise specially prescribed by the said Act, may be made by a Bailiff of the Superior or Circuit Court, whose certificates of service shall be in the form required for service of process in the said Courts ; or by any literate person, who shall certify his service by his affidavit ; and in either case, the manner, place and time of such service shall be described in words, and also the distance from the place of service to the place of proceeding.

18. All services of Writs, Rules, Notices, Warrants or other proceedings, shall be made between the hours of 8 A. M. and 7 P. M., unless otherwise directed by a Judge or Court upon good cause shewn.

19. Writs of Attachment need not be called in open Court, but shall be returned on the return day into the Clerk's Office, and shall be there filed for proceedings thereon, as may be advised or directed.

20. Every day, except Sundays and Holidays, shall be a juridical day for the return of said Writs, and for judicial and Court proceedings.

21. The Sheriff to whom the Writ of Attachment shall be directed, shall not be required to make any detailed Inventory or *procès-verbal* of the effects or articles by him attached under such Writ ; but a full and complete Inventory of the Insolvent's Estate, so attached by the Sheriff, shall be made by the Assignee or

person who shall be placed in possession thereof as guardian under such Writ; by sorting and numbering the books of account, papers, documents and vouchers of the Estate, and entering the same, with the other assets and effects thereof, in detail, in a book for the same, which shall be called " The Inventory of the Estate of ....," and which shall be filed by the said Assignee or person in possession, on the return day of the said Writ, as required by the said Act ; and the said Inventory shall be open for examination or extract at all times during office hours, *gratis*.

22. Immediately upon the execution of the voluntary deed or instrument of assignment to the Assignee, he shall give notice thereof by advertisement in the form D of the said Act, requiring, by such notice, all Creditors of the Insolvent to produce before him, within two months from the date thereof, their claims, specifying the security therefor, with the vouchers in support of such claims, as required by such notice.

23. The Clerk shall prepare for the Judge or Court, a list of matters pending, or ready and fixed for proceeding on each day, following therein the order of procedure prescribed by the 4th Rule, which list shall be communicated to the Judge on the previous day.

24. The record of proceedings in each case shall at all times during office hours, be accessible, at the Clerk's Office, to Creditors and others in interest in such cases, for examination or extract therefrom, *gratis*. And in like manner the minutes of meetings of Creditors, and the registers of proceedings, together with the claims made and the documents in possession of the Assignee, shall also be accessible to Creditors and others in interest in the case, at convenient hours, daily, to be appointed by the said Assignee.

25. The Assignee shall, from time to time, under order of date, and within twenty-four hours after the proceedings had before him, file in the said Clerk's Office, a clear copy under his signature as such Assignee, of such proceedings, together with a copy of the several Newspapers and Official Gazette, in which he shall have caused notices of such proceedings to be advertised, which said copy and newspapers shall form part of the record of proceedings of the particular case.

26. The Assignee shall, on the third juridical day of each month, after he shall have commenced to deposit Estate moneys in a Bank or Bank Agency, as required by the said Act, file of record in the case an account of the Estate, shewing the balance thereof in his hands, or under his control, made up to the last day of the preceding month. And no moneys so deposited, shall be withdrawn without a special order of the Court, entered in the docket of proceedings in the case, or upon a dividend sheet prepared and notified, as required by the said Act, or unless otherwise ordered by the Creditors, under the powers conferred upon them by the said Act.

TARIFF OF FEES IN INSOLVENCY.

ON BEHALF OF THE PLAINTIFFS,

IF NOT CONTESTED:

	$ cts.
To the Prothonotary for Writ of Attachment	1 80
Do. Copy of Writ	0 30
Sheriff for Warrant	2 50
Copies of Warrant, each	0 50
All proceedings by the Sheriff or his Agent or Messenger in the seizure and return, exclusive of Mileage	2 00
Guardian, per day	1 00
Do Making up Inventory and Statements, to be subject to taxation by the Judge :	
To the Prothonotary on return of Writ	5 00
Crier's Fee on Return	0 80
To the Prothonotary for copy of order for meeting	0 50
To the Prothonotary for meeting	1 00
To the Prothonotary for each copy of judgment appointing Official Assignee	0 50
Attorney's Fee for conducting proceedings to appointment of Official Assignee	30 00

IF CONTESTED, ADDITIONAL FEES :

To the Prothonotary on Inscription	2 00
To the Prothonotary on every Witness examined for Plaintiff, exceeding two in number	0 30
And for each subsequent deposition exceeding 400 words in length, for every 100 words	0 10
Attorney's Fee, additional	20 00
Counsel Fee at Enquête	10 00

ON BEHALF OF THE DEFENDANTS,

IF NOT CONTESTED :

Attorney's Fee for appearance	10 00

IF CONTESTED, ADDITIONAL FEES :

To the Prothonotary on filing Petition in contestation	6 00
On every Witness examined for Defendant, exceeding two in number	0 30

7

	$ cts.
And for each subsequent deposition exceeding 400 words in length, for every 100 words	0 10
Attorney's Fee, additional	20 00
Counsel Fee at Enquête	10 00

ON VOLUNTARY ASSIGNMENTS :

To the Prothonotary for filing and entering Deed	2 00

ON PETITIONS, OTHER THAN PETITIONS IN APPEAL, IN CONTESTATION OF PROCEEDINGS FOR COMPULSORY LIQUIDATION, OR FOR EXAMINATION OF DEBTOR :

To the Petitioner's Attorney on every Petition, not contested	5 00
If contested, without Enquête	10 00
If contested, with Enquête	15 00
To the Respondent's Attorney—	
If contested, without Enquête	8 00
If contested, with Enquête	12 00
To the Prothonotary—	
Filing Petitions	2 00
Copy of Order	0 50
If contested, on filing Contestation	2 00
If there be an Enquête, for every deposition	0 30
For all words over 400 in any deposition, per 100	0 10

ON PETITIONS IN APPEAL TO A JUDGE :

To the Assignee for transcript of record and making up record and attendance before the Judge	5 00
To the Prothonotary—	
Filing Petition	2 00
Remission of Record	1 00
To the Attorney for the Petitioner—	
If not contested	10 00
If contested	20 00
To the Attorney for the Respondent	15 00

ON PETITIONS FOR ORDER FOR EXAMINATION OF DEBTOR OR OF OTHER PERSONS RESPECTING THE ESTATE AND EFFECTS OF THE INSOLVENT :

To the Petitioner's Attorney	2 50
To the Prothonotary for order to serve	0 50

ON CLAIMS :

To the Attorneys—	
For every chirographary claim, without security	1 00
For every chirographary claim, with security	2 00
For every hypothecary claim, if not contested	5 00

$ cts.

On every claim contested, without Enquête—
Additional—To Claimant's Attorney.............. 10 00
 To Contestant's Attorney............. 10 00
 With Enquête—
 To Claimant's Attorney.............. 20 00
 To Contestant's Attorney......... ... 20 00
To the Assignee—
 On every chirographary claim and hypothecary claim,
 not contested................................ 0 10
 For every witness examined on the contestation of a
 claim.. 0 25
 On inscription of contestation for argument......... 2 00
On Contestations of Dividend Sheets—
 The same fees and disbursements to Counsel and to
 Assignee as on Contestation of Claim.
On application for discharge by the Court, for confirma-
 tion of discharge, or for annulling discharge :
To the Applicant's Attorney—
 If not contested................................ 15 00
 If contested, without Enquête.................... 25 00
 If contested, with Enquête...................... 35 00
To the Respondent's Attorney—
 If contested, without Enquête.................... 15 00
 If contested, with Enquête...................... 25 00
To the Prothonotary—Filing Application............ 2 00
 Every Deposition.............. 0 30
 All words over 400 in each
 Deposition, per 100......... 0 10

MISCELLANEOUS.

To the Attorneys, Prothonotaries and Bailiffs, Fees and
 disbursements on all Rules, Motions, Copies of
 Rules, Judgments and Orders, Commissions
 rogatoires, and other incidental matters according
 to the same rates as are allowed by the present
 Tariff in first class actions in the Superior Court.
All necessary disbursements for advertisements and notices.

INDEX.

PAGES.

S *

www.ingramcontent.com/pod-product-compliance
Lightning Source LLC
Chambersburg PA
CBHW030621270326
41927CB00007B/1265